Kingston Lacy

Dorset

THE NATIONAL TRUST

1987

Acknowledgements

The National Trust gratefully acknowledges a most
generous grant from the Wolfson Foundation which made
possible the restoration of Rubens' *Marchese Caterina
Grimaldi* for 'The Treasure Houses of Britain'
exhibition in Washington in 1985.

The late Daphne Bankes transcribed letters and
documents in the Library and Muniment Room at
Kingston Lacy in the 1930s which have been invaluable.
Hugh Jacques and his staff at the Dorchester Record
Office, where the Bankes archives are being catalogued,
have been of the greatest help. Research has been
undertaken there by William Riviere, Anthony Kilroy
and John Cornforth, in his usual illuminating manner.
Antony Cleminson unravelled the architectural history
of the house and built the models in the exhibition room.
St John Gore and Alastair Laing have catalogued the
pictures.

A.M.

Lely's portrait of *Sir Ralph Bankes* is by courtesy
of the Yale Center for British Art, Paul Mellon Fund and
William Bankes in Oriental Dress is by courtesy of the
Searight Collection, Trustees of the Victoria
and Albert Museum.

Cover: Kingston Lacy engraved by Philip Brannon, 1860s.

Photographs by: Richard Pink, Royal Studios, Wimborne
and the Courtauld Institute.

Designed by James Shurmer

Printed in England by The Stellar Press, Hatfield, Herts

Contents

Kingston Lacy

Sir John Bankes the able lawyer and Charles I's Chief Justice purchased Corfe Castle in 1635 and the old royal estate of Kingston Lacy in 1632–36. While he attended the King in Oxford Lady Bankes withstood two sieges at Corfe, which was only taken by treachery in 1646, the Roundhead colonel saluting her courage by permitting her to depart with the keys of the Castle which still hang in the Library at Kingston Lacy. Corfe was 'slighted' by Parliament and its picturesque ruin still evokes the most poignant memorial of the Royalist cause.

At the Restoration Sir Ralph Bankes was knighted by Charles II and built a new family seat, Kingston Hall, near the site of the medieval manor house which had disappeared a hundred and fifty years before. He employed Sir Roger Pratt as his architect from 1663–65, whose one surviving drawing shows an endearing example of the red brick Caroline house, with stone quoins, pediment, hipped roof and cupola, evolved by this gentleman architect who contributed to 'the politer way of living'. Sir Ralph's collection of pictures is one of the earliest made by the gentry.

Henry Bankes, scholar and parliamentarian, remodelled the house with his archi-

Kingston Lacy, the North Front and East Loggia

The South Front

tect R. F. Brettingham on his return from Rome in the 1780s. His surviving rooms are the Library and the Saloon with its painted ceiling. He also enlarged the park to its present shape and carried out extensive planting.

His son William John Bankes, the boon companion of Byron at Cambridge, collected pictures in Spain in 1812–14, travelled widely in Syria and made two expeditions up the Nile to Abu Simbel and beyond, acquiring the obelisk from Philae. On his way home in 1820 he bought important pictures in Bologna and visited Byron in Ravenna. He rebuilt his Welsh house Soughton in 1820–21 with some help from Charles Barry whom he met in Egypt. From 1835–41 they transformed Kingston Hall into the house we know today, encased in Chilmark stone, with a new cupola and balustrade and a Roman staircase of Carrara marble reaching the state rooms via a loggia in the style of Inigo Jones. In 1841 he was prosecuted for a breach of sexual convention and went to live abroad, where he devoted himself to designing and commissioning the fittings in marble and wood, which his Italian craftsmen carved. He continued to ship these over, with prolific and precise instructions to his clerk of works Osborne and his mason Seymour, until his death in 1855 in Venice. Kingston Lacy, as the house now came to be called, is his monument and the Spanish Room his golden masterpiece.

Further changes were made by the late Mr Ralph Bankes' parents who were married in 1897. In 1981 Mr Bankes bequeathed the Corfe Castle and Kingston Lacy estates to the National Trust.

Plan of the House

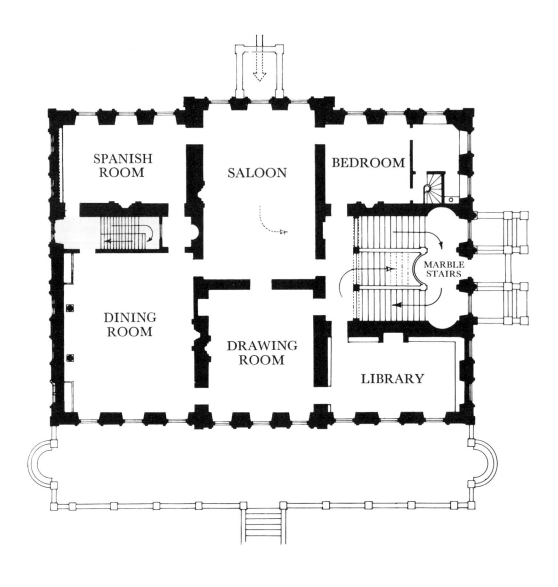

SPANISH ROOM

SALOON

BEDROOM

DINING ROOM

DRAWING ROOM

MARBLE STAIRS

LIBRARY

N

Principal floor as altered by Charles Barry in 1835–40.
Researched and drawn by Antony Cleminson, Grad. Dipl. Cons. (AA).

Tour of the House

The Entrance Hall

William Bankes (1786–1855) formed a new Entrance Hall at basement level by lowering the ground eight feet on the north side of the house and added the *porte cochère* to Barry's design in the 1830s. The Hall, though rather low and dark, is dignified by Doric columns and a compartmented ceiling enlivened with egg and dart moulding and guilloche ornament. Bankes saw this kind of sub-hall when he visited Amesbury Abbey, another house thought at the time to be by Inigo Jones.

Sculpture

The pair of tables were ordered by Bankes in Italy with his 'oriental red granite' tops, and these are perhaps 'the four table legs with fruits' sculpted by Salesio Pegrassi in white Verona marble described in 1849. They have scrolled supports on paw feet and the sides are carved with shells, fruit, a lizard and a moth.

The pair of composition basket *jardinières* in the windows were shipped from Venice in 1846. The terracotta *jardinières*, modelled on the two bronze wellheads in the court-yard of the Doge's palace in Venice, were contracted for 'twelve gold Napoleons' by Angelo Giordani in July 1848 – he was still at work on them in August 1852 when Bankes threatened to prosecute if he did not finish them promptly. Above, on the left-hand side, is a superb marble portrait bust, supposed by the family to be of Sir John Bankes (1589–1644) of Corfe Castle, the Lord Chief Justice, but the sculpture, Roman baroque of the early seventeenth century, hardly represents him and it is unlikely that Sir John sat to a sculptor in the circle of Algardi or Fanelli, nor do we know that he visited Rome. It has been suggested that possibly he or his sons might have sent his rather conventional portrait in the Library to a Roman sculptor, following Charles I's example with Bernini, although the bust, set up here in 1913 by the late Mr Bankes' mother, does not appear in the nineteenth-century inventories of the house.

Below the bust is a collection of French and Venetian bronze door furniture dating from the fifteenth to the eighteenth centuries – the blackamoor heads must have attracted Bankes because the family crest is a moor's head with a cap of maintenance adorned with a crescent and a fleur de lys. The ebony cabinet is late seventeenth-century Flemish and opposite stands a George III black and gold lacquer cabinet. The tall bronze cranes are nineteenth-century Japanese.

Beyond the screen the Inner Hall is dominated by the large chimneypiece, carved with irises, lilies and William Bankes' coat of arms (sable, a cross engrailed ermine, between four fleur de lys or), quartered with Wynne and Brune, and the family motto

Barry's Entrance Hall

Velle Quod Vult Deus (Desire what God wishes). Below stand a fine pair of late sixteenth-century Venetian bronze andirons, surmounted by expressive female figures in the style of Alessandro Vittoria. The *torchères* or 'candelabra' either side are probably by Pegrassi and finely carved in *Biancone*, one with fir and holly and the other with holly and ivy, and small birds. This hard Italian stone-coloured marble comes from Bassano and Bankes used it throughout the house for carved decoration. The pair of oval brass urns, or tazzas, are probably from the workshop of Baron Marochetti and cast in relief with battle scenes, winged masks and serpent handles. They stand on 'two open-work stoves in Carrara marble' (radiator covers), contracted for by Pietro Lorandini in June 1850, and bearing the Greek inscription ʼΑΡΙΣΤΟΝ ΜΕΝ ʽΥΔΩΡ (Water is best). Their centres are inset with bronze medallions ordered from Marochetti in October 1853 when the sculptor visited Bankes in Paris with 'his two most beautiful daguerreotypes' for them. 'Nothing can be so perfect, or so completely as I could have wished' he wrote to his sister Lady Falmouth. The one on the right shows Kingston Hall in its original state, with Pratt's plan for the principal floor.

The Marble Staircase

There are careful measured drawings by Barry for the Carrara marble stairs and he surely succeeded in satisfying William Bankes' desire to build a staircase worthy of an Italian *palazzo*, ascending to the state rooms on the first floor or *piano nobile*, and above. The perspective is heightened by the descent of the vault against the ascent of the staircase to the loggia. Bankes most admired the staircase in the Palazzo Ruspoli in Rome, but the idea of the loggia was Barry's. In December 1837 he wrote to his brother George 'I am astonished at the rate of progress of the works, and more than ever pleased with them, the Lantern is everything that I could wish, and so is the drawing room ceiling, that is to say their effect is exactly what it was upon paper – but the staircase turns out *far beyond* it (if staircase it may be called that stairs has none), it is now formed and roughed out in almost every part, all the openings clear, and all the ceilings shaped so that proportions, and perspectives, and distribution, and lighting, can all be judged of quite as well as can ever be, and I must pronounce (though it cannot be said *impartially*) that so far as my judgement goes, there is no staircase in England equal to it in effect, not even Wardour, and not many that surpass it in Italy. I delight in the rich Eastern external Loggia which is finished, but I do nothing but walk up and down the inclined planes of the Staircase.'

The first flight arrives on a half-landing at the airy loggia and garden entrance on the east, looking out into the park over the 'Dutch garden', laid out at the turn of the century. In the 1830s Barry, with one of his most attractive drawings, proposed a more extravagant scheme with raised walks, a large conservatory, fountains and other structures. The cedars beyond were planted by Bankes in 1835 as part of a projected 'green drive' to Pamphill village. One of Barry's drawings shows the loggia glazed with bars but Bankes later refers to the 'two great plates of glass required on the first landing of the marble stairs', and writing to Osborne as late as December 1848, '. . . I propose to have these up next season'. Were they perhaps first glazed as shown in the drawing and later fitted with plate glass?

Bronze

In the loggia are two more pairs of brass urns with masks, one with snakes for handles, the other with fruit. The three monumental bronze figures mounted impressively over the radiator grilles in their shell niches portray Sir John Bankes, Lady Bankes and King Charles I. These were commissioned by William Bankes from Baron Marochetti (1805–1867), the Turin-born French sculptor, who first came to England in 1848. His work may also be seen at Salisbury, Stratfield Saye, Belton, Frogmore and Glasgow, where Bankes was instrumental in obtaining for Marochetti the commission for the equestrian statue of the Duke of Wellington erected in 1844. Although it was in his mind from the early 1840s, he only signed a contract with the sculptor in Paris on 18 November 1853 for the special bargain price of £2,500 (which was to be kept secret) for the three figures 'to be finished and in place within two years from this date'. Brave Dame Mary, her face faithfully portraying 'her character of firmness and determination' based on the enamel by Bone and the original miniature (both in the Drawing Room) sent up to the Baron's studio in Onslow Square by Lady Falmouth at her brother's request, holds her sword and the key of Corfe Castle. Below the king the bronze relief shows the siege in full swing – 'it must be *extremely* accurate' wrote Bankes of the castle. He wrote again to his sister from Venice, almost for the last time, in March 1855: 'I scarcely ever received a letter that gave me more pleasure than one which reached me the day before yesterday from Marochetti, enclosing a photograph, (which you know is a reduced representation produced mechanically on paper, and therefore exact to the utmost degree), of the basrelief executed by him, or under his eye, from my drawing, he seems to be delighted with the success of it, as well he may be. . . . If the execution of the statues be conformable to this high standard of excellence (as no doubt it will be), where will there be in any private house in England a family monument of equal magnificence?' He never saw the finished statues in place and they were not paid for until some time after his death.

Sculpture

The second flight reaches the *piano nobile* at a landing with three domes and five doorways of finely carved *Biancone di Bassano*, three of them pedimented. This beautiful marble was carved by Salesio Pegrassi of Verona into the pair of 'candelabra' either side of the Saloon doors, designed by William Bankes and described in a newspaper extract from the *Foglio di Verona* of 27 September 1849 devoted to the sculptor and 'his well deserved English Maecenas'. One is wreathed with olive and the other with myrtle, sacred to Minerva the goddess of learning and to Venus the goddess of love. The medallion of Minerva was taken from an impression of a gem by Marchant in the Library sent over to Bankes in Italy. The 'two exquisite terms' – tapering bird figures – opposite were shipped home in April 1854 and are probably Pegrassi's work also. From the left the doors lead into the Library, the Drawing Room, the Saloon and the State Bedroom. The last door but one was filled with a slab of grey marble on which is recorded the building history of the house, Inigo Jones being credited as the original architect because the family had long forgotten Sir Roger Pratt's involvement. Over the State Bedroom doorcase is a nineteenth-century bust of Marcus Agrippa and over the Library doorcase is 'an antique bust of Augustus mounted to match exactly' in 1847, over the inscription *Lateritiam Accepi Marmoream Reliqui* (I found it of brick and left it of marble) from Suetonius writing of Augustus and the city of Rome.

Lady Bankes by Baron Marochetti

The Library

The Library was originally divided into a withdrawing room and Sir Ralph Bankes' closet. In its present form the room dates from the time of William Bankes' father, Henry Bankes (1757–1834), who employed the architect Robert Furze Brettingham (c.1750–1820, grandson of Matthew Brettingham senior), whom he met on his second visit to Rome in 1782, to make extensive alterations to the house on his return. The drawing for the bookcases, either by Brettingham or by an Italian decorator, is at Kingston Lacy. The Library was one of the last rooms William Bankes intended to transform and detailed drawings were made for heightening and embellishing the ceiling, to frame the Tintoretto flanked by two paintings by 'Bonifacio' bought in Venice in 1849. The work 'had been in hand five years under my eye' when he abandoned the scheme to please his sister Lady Falmouth who had come to live at Kingston Lacy as a widow. Their affectionate correspondence survives and he writes from Venice in May 1854 'As I am continually thinking of you, and having so few objects left, my desire is to make you comfortable, and your residence at Kingston Lacy more and more acceptable to you. . . . I have therefore at once decided on counter ordering it all, and can assure you in all sincerity that I feel more actual pleasure and satisfaction in doing so from such a motive, . . . than I could possibly have felt from carrying out my plans. . . . I will show you that my hands are full of something else, for I will at once turn them to a room with which you can have no associations . . .'

During his grand tour of 1778–80 Henry Bankes reluctantly sat in 1779, on his mother's insistence, to Batoni, the painter of so many young English 'milordi' in Rome, and the portrait hangs on the window wall. He did not think Batoni's portraits equal to those of Reynolds, writing to his mother on 24 November 1779 '. . . I believe it will be finished tomorrow or the next day. . . . It is certainly like me, but without any sort of Taste or good painting'. It was shipped home in 1780, after alterations, when he wrote again 'I wish much it may please you when you receive it better than it does me, for I think it but a melancholy cold picture whose only merit is being simple and having nothing offensive.'

The Library itself has hardly changed in content since Henry's death in 1834. While including some of his son William's expensive folios, notably the *Description de l'Egypt* (1809–1828) and the picaresque memoirs of Giovanni Finati his travelling companion in the Middle East, which he published in 1830, many of the better bound volumes reflect Henry's classical education in literature and history. The core of the Library, however, is that of the seventeenth-century Civil War family, including two books which belonged to Sir Nicholas Bacon, one with an elaborate armorial binding by Jean de Planche, and presumably to Sir John Bankes himself, whose own library must have largely perished or been scattered after the siege of Corfe Castle. His portrait in judge's robes is on the window wall. His sons travelled on the Continent

The Library

for their education during the Commonwealth. John, the eldest son who died young, signed his acquisitions in France and Italy, and Ralph, the builder of the house, may have collected the seventeenth-century engraved architectural volumes. Jerome, the third son, travelled as far as Naples, where he was painted, unusually for a young Englishman, by Stanzione, and his portrait hangs over the chimneypiece.

Pictures

Above the bookcases hang Lely's portraits of this generation who came into their own at the Restoration of the monarchy in 1660. Sir Ralph Bankes (?1631–1677), who employed the architect Sir Roger Pratt to build the new house for the family at Kingston Lacy in 1663–65, is on the far wall and three of his beautiful sisters, Lady Jenkinson, Lady Cullen and Mrs Gilly, are on the fireplace wall. Arabella, on the right, married Samuel Gilly of High Hall, a nearby house contemporary with Kingston Hall, which was later bought in 1691 by John Fitch, brother of the brickwork contractor who built Kingston Hall under Pratt's direction, and which still remains in the possession of his descendants. According to Bankes' family tradition, Lely stayed in the house to paint the family. Sir Joshua Reynolds when he visited the house with Dr Johnson in 1762, noted in his journal 'I never had fully appreciated Sir Peter Lely till I had seen these portraits'. At that time they were hung next door in the great parlour (now the Drawing Room), and their present arrangement is due to Henry Bankes (although there is no inventory from his time). His son William wrote 'It were to be wished that the Library could accommodate a greater number of books, but the fine family portraits are admirably placed in it, and I should be at a loss how to dispose them elsewhere.' The Sunderland frames of 'Mr Stafford' and Lady Jenkinson and her two sisters are original and the others, perhaps carved for the eighteenth-century collection, were altered for William in the nineteenth century 'to correspond'.

Sir Joshua also wrote to Boswell, Samuel Johnson's biographer, 'Those motions or tricks of Dr Johnson are improperly called convulsions. . . . When he and I took a journey together into the West, we visited the late Mr Banks, of Dorsetshire; the conversation turning upon pictures, which Johnson could not well see, he retired to a corner of the room, stretching out his right leg as far as he could reach before him, then bringing up his left leg, and stretching his right still further on. The old gentleman [the bachelor John Bankes whose portrait is on the window wall] observing him, went up to him, and in a very courteous manner assured him, that though it was not a new house, the flooring was perfectly safe. The Doctor started from his reverie, like a person waked out of his sleep, but spoke not a word.'

Furniture

Over the chimneypiece are the keys of Corfe Castle, which Lady Bankes was allowed to retain as a mark of her courage, with a spur and cannon-balls from the siege. Next to the keys hang 'one hundred impressions of gems' engraved with antique statues in Rome by Nathaniel Marchant (1739–1816) for wealthy English travellers. Henry Bankes and Sir Richard Colt Hoare were among his patrons for these gems and similar impressions of them are in the library at Stourhead. Henry wrote of his seal 'cut to great perfection by Marchant'. The Regency rosewood writing table with brass edges and fluted splayed feet is in the manner of John McLean and Son, the London firm of cabinet-makers active in the early years of the nineteenth century, who furnished and upholstered Middleton Park, Oxfordshire for the Earl of Jersey in 1806–7, but went bankrupt in the 1820s. The carpet of a 'Persian design' was supplied by S. R. Whitty of Axminster on 12 October 1819 for £60.16.0 and is one of a group of Axminster carpets, including that in the Spanish Room, purchased by Henry Bankes from Samuel Whitty between 1818 and 1824.

The Drawing Room

Sir Ralph Bankes' great parlour of the 1660s became the Drawing Room in the 1780s and Henry Bankes' chimneypiece and doors survive from this time. Barry raised the ceiling in the 1830s and the design is from a ceiling at Lees Court, Kent, another 'Inigo Jones' house visited by William Bankes. The original ceiling was destroyed in the fire at Lees Court in 1910 but is recorded in a drawing of 1838 still at Kingston Lacy. The stencil for the Bankes motto *Velle Quod Vult Deus* along the frieze was sent from Venice in 1846. The pair of console tables either side of the great doors to the Saloon are carved 'in pale Sienna marble, excepting the medallion which will be of black and inlaid with *pietra dura* in colour, a lion's head to be substituted for the mask' from a drawing made by Bankes, 'an exact copy from the original by the famous Ammanati of Florence'. He also had an alabaster model made at Lucca. An estimate for the marble at 170 *scudi* and for making the tables for 540 *scudi* in seventy-five working days was given by Antonio Ferrari of Rome in October 1844. The four door architraves of the yellow marble of Torre were executed in Verona by Michelangelo Montrésor in 1846, as were those in the Dining Room and the Saloon, and the 'Great

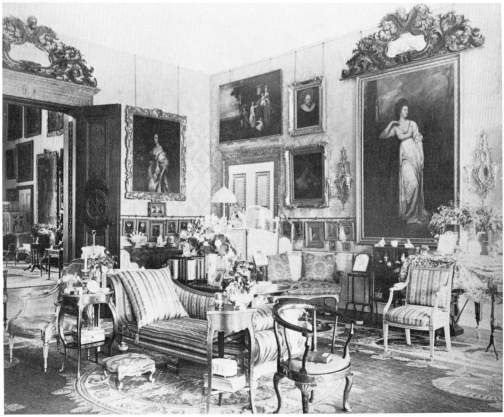

The Drawing Room photographed in 1900 by *The Ladies' Field*

Door for the Hall 10′ 6″ high by 5′ 6″ wide of yellow Torre with jambs' is referred to in July of the same year. The three large scrolled crestings with the cypher W.J.B., like those in the Dining Room, are called 'Bavarian' by William Bankes.

Furniture

The Drawing Room is, however, essentially the creation of the late Mr Bankes' mother and it retains the character of a cluttered Edwardian drawing room, captured by *The Ladies' Field* in the photograph of 1900. Henrietta Jenny Fraser married Walter Ralph Bankes in 1897 but was left a widow in 1904 with two daughters and a small son. She managed the estate and ran the house for many years, entertaining royalty, planting the garden, and recording all the improvements carried out during her reign in a book. Photographs of her are on the Carlton House inlaid desk and a watercolour of her and her eldest daughter Daphne, painted in 1902 by Mary Gow, hangs on the right of the chimneypiece. She re-covered the walls in rose damask the year after her marriage and covered the sofa and chairs in green striped silk, both from Haynes of Spring Street, Paddington. As the previous drawing room furniture had been removed to London and dispersed 'by a previous Mrs Bankes' she completely refurnished the room, exept for the *secretaire à abattant* with the porcelain plaque which was in the Saloon in 1856, the black boys balancing flower tubs on their feet, and the sofa tables. The nineteenth-century French furniture and late Dresden china is typical of the taste of 1900, surrounded by work boxes, miniatures and plenty of luxuriant plants. The screen and the piano stool on lyre supports and covered in painted velvet came from her own town house. The carpet is a Savonnerie of about 1830, rather later in date than the Saloon carpet.

Pictures

Lawrence's portrait of William Bankes' favourite sister, Lady Falmouth, is over the door on the right of the chimneypiece. The correspondence between William and his sister seems to be the only personal one to survive among his largely business papers and after she came to live at Kingston Lacy as a widow he relied on her judgement and reports on the progress of the work of the fitting up and decoration of the rooms which, after 1841, he was obliged to conduct by remote, but firm, control from his exile in Italy. At the far end of the room hang the pair of Van Dycks of Sir John and Lady Borlase; she was the eldest daughter of Sir John and Lady Bankes and portraits of three of her sisters by Lely are in the Library.

A closer view of the Van Dycks and some of the Bone enamels may be enjoyed from the Saloon doorway later in the tour.

Romney's full-length portrait of Frances Woodley, 'one of the most remarkable beauties of the day', wife of Henry Bankes and mother of William, hangs opposite

Lady Jenkinson by Lely   *Lady Borlase* by Van Dyck

the fireplace. *The Gentleman's Magazine* reported 'This lady in 1781 shone at Bath in the first circles of fashion; she drew all eyes and warmed all hearts.' The same year she sat to Romney, before her marriage in 1784. On his travels William Bankes wrote from Cairo in 1815 'Tell my mother that I never ceased to think of her among the figs and mulberries of Mount Sinai.' Either side of her are two portraits by Lawrence: her sister Maria, Mrs Ridell, who counted Robert Burns and Henry Fuseli among her many admirers, and Mrs Johnstone, later Lady Nugent, her second son George's mother-in-law, and mistress of the Duke of Cumberland, who brought royal blood into the Bankes family.

Miniatures

Below the paintings are a collection of fifty-five enamel miniatures painted on copper by Henry Bone (1755–1834) portraying Queen Elizabeth and her courtiers and contemporaries. Queen Elizabeth sold Corfe to Sir Christopher Hatton, from whose daughter-in-law, Lady Coke, Sir John Bankes purchased the castle in 1635; all these except Lady Coke are among Bone's subjects. Henry Bone was the son of a Cornish cabinet-maker, employed as a boy by William Cookworthy to decorate the new Plymouth hard paste porcelain, and then in Bristol. After he went to London and became an Academician in 1811, he developed large miniature painting on enamel and first exhibited fifty-four Elizabethans at his house at 15 Berners Street in 1822, adding to them over the years and also portraying distinguished people in the reign of Charles I. These at Kingston Lacy, copied from paintings in well-known houses, were mostly acquired by William Bankes in 1836 after the artist's death, and the architect Vulliamy, who worked for him in the London house, 5 Old Palace Yard, seems to have acted as agent for their purchase. There is no longer one of Byron but there are two of Lady Bankes, of whom there is no other portrait in the house, except for the miniature in the showcase from which Bone copied them. The portraits of Sir John and Lady Bankes at Sudbury, Derbyshire, were inherited from Lady Borlase, whose great-great-granddaughter married the 4th Lord Vernon. Lady Bankes' parents, Mary Altham and Ralph Hawtrey of Ruislip, hang above the Lawrences and closely resemble the portrait busts by John and Matthias Christmas on their monument in Ruislip church.

The Dining Room

The present Dining Room was made by Barry in the 1830s when Brettingham's family staircase was removed and the space thrown into the south-west apartment, one of four suites, consisting of a square room and one or two closets, placed by Pratt at the corners of the house. We know the south-west apartment had survived as Mr and Mrs Henry Bankes' bedroom and dressing rooms from her account of the ball they gave in 1791, after the alterations by Brettingham had swept away the partitions in the other three corners to create the Library, the eating room and the north parlour (*see plans* p.56). Barry was obliged to replace the load-bearing wall by a huge steel joist and what the Trust's architects called 'a veritable card-castle of trusses', which came to light during the repairs of 1982–84. The need for a larger dining room for entertaining had been felt for some time, for there are a number of drawings by various architects for extending the eating room in the north-west, notably by Wyatville in 1821. One such scheme was actually carried out before William Bankes adopted Barry's solution.

Barry's ceiling is inspired by those at Coleshill, which was Sir Roger Pratt's last remaining unaltered house until its destruction by fire in 1953, and the drawings Barry made for Bankes of the ceilings there are still at Kingston Lacy. He owned a Rubens tapestry cartoon, *The Triumph of Divine Love*, from which he considered having an oval of putti cut out to go in the centre of this ceiling, but the cartoon survived and went to Soughton, his Welsh house. Unfortunately a fire here in the Dining Room in the nineteenth century damaged the decorations and only the ceiling, the highly carved crestings above the windows, the carved walnut shutters for which working drawings exist from Bankes' own designs, and the four pairs of carved boxwood doors survive. After the fire Walter Ralph Bankes (1853–1904) panelled the room in oak and cedarwood grown in the park. The organ was moved here from the Saloon where it had been above the large doors into the Drawing Room and played from a console within the Drawing Room cupboard doors. The *Judgement of Solomon*, originally hung opposite the chimneypiece in the Saloon, was moved to its present position in the Dining

The Judgement of Solomon

Room at the same time, where it is well placed with the light falling correctly from the left.

The Judgement of Solomon

The great unfinished masterpiece *The Judgement of Solomon*, now attributed to Sebastiano del Piombo but long thought to be the work of Giorgione, draws the eye into the room. The story of Solomon's wisdom told in the first Book of Kings, chapter three, verses 16–28, is shown with the true mother on the right painted in a gesture of sacrifice: 'O my Lord, give her the living child, and in no wise slay it. But the other said, Let it be neither mine nor thine, but divide it.' And so the king found the true mother and gave her the living baby. The false mother whose baby had died is on the left, but the executioner on the extreme right has no sword and both babies are also missing because the painting was never finished. Recent cleaning and infra-red photography have revealed not only the sword and the babies but at least two incomplete compositions, one on top of the other on the same canvas, as can be discerned in the architectural setting. The later setting shows familiarity with the judicial implications of the antique or early Christian basilica, but the king's throne is brought forward and not placed in the apse. Thus, although a learned painting, the artist has freed himself from archaeology to lay out his masterly and spacious composition with lucid narrative coherence.

The Judgement of Solomon was painted in about 1505–10. The first surviving reference to it is by Ridolfi who saw it in 1648 in the Palazzo Vendramin-Calergi, as it is now known, built before 1509 by the wealthy official Andrea Loredan, who died in battle in 1513. It has been suggested that this judicial scene was commissioned by Loredan for a public position in the Doge's palace but taken to his own residence because it was left unfinished when Sebastiano left Venice for Rome in 1511. It may well have remained in the great *Salone* on the first floor, like other paintings, when the Loredan family sold the palace in 1581, for it belonged there to the subsequent owners of the palace, the Grimani-Calergi family, but does not appear in the sixteenth-century inventories of the Grimani collections.

William Bankes, returning home through Italy to see his friend Byron after eight years of travelling in Spain and the Middle East, heard the painting was for sale early in 1820. Explaining his delay in Bologna he asked Byron in Ravenna for his opinion of the picture. Byron replied on 26 February 1820 '. . . I know nothing of pictures myself, and care almost as little : but to me there are none like the Venetian – above all, Giorgione. I remember well his Judgment of Solomon in the Mariscalchi in Bologna. The real mother is beautiful, exquisitely beautiful. Buy her, by all means, if you can, and take her home with you : put her in safety : for be assured there are troublous times brewing for Italy ; and as I never could keep out of a row in my life, it will be my fate, I dare say, to be over head and ears in it ; but no matter, these are the stronger reasons for coming to see me soon'.

Marescalchi's receipt for '. . . il Judicio di Salomone non finito de Giorgione di Castel Franco' for 575 *scudi* is dated Bologna 11 January 1820, so it seems Bankes had already made up his mind to acquire the painting even without Byron's encouragement. His mother noted in her diary on 8 February that a letter from William in Bologna 'has horrified his father, having drawn £500 to pay for unfinished pictures of masters that he does not fancy'.

Furniture

Below the *Judgement* stands an Italian pokerwork coffer in cedarwood of the late sixteenth century, the cartouche on the top is inscribed 'Barbarus Hyde'. On the right of the organ hangs a verdure tapestry, acquired by W.R.Bankes, depicting Apollo and Daphne. English, and dating from the early eighteenth century, it was probably woven in Soho. Below it is

'*A Large Mahogany Semi Oval Sideboard Curiously*
Inlaid with Various different Colour'd Woods. Composing
Ornaments of Virtruvian Scrole border. Cross banded &
Strung on top. the frieze border'd with running flowers
& on therm'd pannell'd feet. decorated with falls of leaves
the whole Richly Engraved . . .'

purchased by Henry Bankes on 30 August 1786 from Ince and Mayhew of Broad Street, Soho for £29.18.3, including the 'Patent Oil Cloth Cover for the top . . . lined with green baize & bound with green Silk binding £1.1.–'. On the sideboard is a display of the Bankes' family silver. Over the first doorway is a portrait of the 2nd Duke of Ormonde whose grandfather the 1st Duke of Ormonde lived at Kingston Lacy as tenant after the death of Sir Ralph Bankes until he died in the house in 1688. The two stained limewood pendant appliques, richly carved in the style of Grinling Gibbons with game, fruit and foliage, have recently been returned from the Saloon to this room where they were in 1860. The composite Roman baroque giltwood console is made up from several pieces, on a bronzed base carved with crouching athletes,

(*Left*) The Boxwood Doors – detail. (*Right*) An 'exquisite term' in *Biancone* on the staircase

supporting a scalloped shell, dolphins and seated trumpeting tritons flanking a figure of Flora with a cornucopia. Two of these ten-feet-high pieces were intended to complement the design of the largest Gobelins tapestry in the Saloon.

The two early seventeenth-century Roman carved walnut *cassoni*, or marriage chests, were acquired by Bankes in Italy. 'Barrini accepts the offer of 500 L.A. [Austrian Lire] for the two yellow vases – *tutto compresso*' noted Bankes in June 1853, of the pair carved in Torre marble with lion skins, bearded masks and vine leaves, which rest on the chimneypiece of the same material. Bartholomeo Barrini acknowledged the final payment the following April. The set of eighteen William IV mahogany dining chairs are covered in giraffe hide. The Victorian chandelier by F. and C. Osler of Birmingham was acquired at the Milton Abbey sale in 1932. While it was being fixed remnants of painting on the ceiling were recorded here.

The Boxwood Doors

The panels of the four pairs of double doors were carved in boxwood by Vincenzo Favenza in Venice between 1849 and 1853 and are fully documented by Bankes, from his first thoughts about the subject matter to details of Favenza's progress and accounts paid for the work. He wrote from Venice in April 1853 'The four folding doors in carved boxwood for the great dining room are the uninterrupted work of four years, and I consider them the finest things yet sent over, as well as the costliest, for, with their marble architraves when up, and in place, – £1000 would do little more than pay for them'. From Paris in September 1853 he wrote '*all* is copied from the finest models that exist wherever they were to be found. . . . Of the panels with Cupids playing on different instruments, or singing, eleven are from the works of Donatello in Padua, one – (that which beats the drum) from a little bronze statue by Sansovino in the Frioul, and four from the alto-relievos of Luca della Robbia in Florence. Of the heads – that of Bacchus is after Sansovino. Pomona from the antique statue in the Florence gallery. One of the young Fauns from the Capitol at Rome, the other from an antique colossal head at Venice, where also is its female companion. The bearded Faun and the bearded Bacchus from Greek antiques in the Grimani collection in Venice. The treatment and attire of the Ceres from an Empress (in the character of Ceres) at Venice, and her head from the medals of Syracuse.'

The Coffee Loggia

One pair of the carved doors leads into this entirely successful small room created by Barry for William Bankes and accessible also from the Spanish Room. It has a vaulted ceiling ingeniously lit by a lamp above the alabaster boss and two niches with shell heads above a pair of fixed console tables carved in *Biancone* by Michelangelo Montrésor sent from Verona to Venice in 1845. The 'floor of inlaid woods' was embarked with the tables but 'still not laid down' in December 1848 and instructions were given to Osborne to be sure to have it laid next season. The Coffee Loggia is a delightful example of Barry's flair as a designer and his skilful use of space behind the backstairs, from which light is borrowed through the alabaster niche and increased by mirror glass.

The Saloon

The ante room, or double height hall, of Pratt's original house had a large gallery or '*pergolo*' at the south end which made the hall itself into a cube. It was taken down early in the eighteenth century, when Pratt's cornice was extended round the south end. In 1762 the room was called the great hall with pictures hung above and below the cornice. It became the Saloon or Ballroom early in Henry Bankes' time when, influenced perhaps by his Dorset neighbours at Milton Abbey and Bryanston, he employed the architect Robert Furze Brettingham on his return from Rome in 1782 to build the coved ceiling and the existing cornice and frieze. Such grand rooms with painted ceilings by Wyatt and others were the fashion in Dorset at this period, as at Crichel and Lulworth. There are vouchers for some of Brettingham's craftsmen, including a number in 1790 for painting by Cornelius Dixon who is recorded as an 'ornament painter' at Strawberry Hill and 15 St James' Square in the 1790s, so it was probably he who painted the ceiling. Flaxman was paid £66 6s for chimney-pieces in March 1786 before he went to Italy the following year and this in the Saloon must be his. William Bankes wrote 'the Saloon and Library I have preserved as altered by my father whose architect was Brettingham (one of the best of a very bad and flimsy time) – the raising the central window of the saloon was happy and though the frieze and the cove might have been better, they are not much to be found fault with, and the Saloon is a room of noble and inspiring effect upon the whole. I never remember it as originally with its flat ceiling and gallery across the end, but believe it must be handsomer altogether as it is.'

William Bankes, according to his notebook for the years 1836–40, intended the Saloon walls to be hung with the Gobelins tapestries he had previously acquired for his Welsh house, Soughton, together with the four 'Carraccis' painted on cloth which are now in the Dining Room. This explains why the Saloon walls appeared to have been prepared for a fabric when they were investigated in 1984 before repainting. He wrote 'If the Saloon be all tapestry . . .' and again 'The sole difficulty of my transferring my Gobelins hither from Soughton arises from the immense size of the great piece'. This is the large 'Triumph of Venus' from the series *Les Triomphes des Dieux* woven at the Gobelins in the late seventeenth century, with Neptune in the foreground riding the waves in a shell chariot drawn by seahorses accompanied by nymphs and tritons. These joyful creatures were to be complemented in the design of the two made-up gilt baroque pieces of furniture, one of which survives in the Dining Room. The tapestries remained at Soughton, inherited by William's younger brother Edward Bankes and his descendants, until they were sold in 1976. In 1844 William wrote to his brother George about the 'Carraccis' '. . . it will be a matter for consideration whether they and the Gobelins tapestry will not ultimately be transferred to Soughton where the room was built for them. The Saloon, which had been got ready for their reception being now hung with oil pictures.'

Pictures

The Bankes' family collection of pictures has always been the chief interest at Kingston Lacy and includes one of the earliest surviving groups collected by a member of the gentry. In 1659, before he built the house, Sir Ralph listed thirty-six pictures in 'A Noate of my Pictures att Grayes Inn and what they cost'. Some fourteen of these can be identified in the collection today. These include 'A Magdalen of Mr. Lillys £20', the two large mythological scenes by Bourdon, £20 each, and 'A Greate Landskip of Bergens' bought from Lely for £33, 'painted to order in Harlem in 1658', all in the Saloon. '. . . it is curious', commented William Bankes, 'that he had bought several (in Cromwell's or R. Cromwell's time) of the king's pictures (which he calls Mantua Pictures) of the regicide Harrison, so that it is evident he had made up his mind to that state of things' – but the four listed in 1659 as bought from Harrison cannot be identified. John Bankes, the bachelor who inherited in 1714 and welcomed Reynolds to Kingston Lacy, paid 'Mr George Dowdney Painter in full for lining, cleaning, mending and varnishing all my pictures at Kingston Hall' £56 13s in December 1731, which tallies with the figure at the end of a list of 128 pictures. He bought Lady Rooke's portrait by Dahl for two guineas in 1738. An inventory of 1762 made for John by his brother Henry lists twenty-three pictures in the Great Hall including the Van Dycks and 'Mr. Edward Altham, in a Pilgrim's Habit – Painted at Rome, by Salvator Rosa' still in the room.

Henry Bankes bought paintings, such as the *Martyrdom of St Stephen* (No.67), but not on the scale or with the flair of his son William, whose dazzling acquisitions both during his father's lifetime, like the 'Raphael', the 'Giorgione' and the Titian, and later, the pair of Rubenses, displaced some of the duller seventeenth-century paintings to the backstairs and attics.

William's 'Raphael', *The Holy Family with St John* (No.42), the first picture low down on the chimneypiece wall, is attributed to his pupil Giulio Romano and shows the artist's awareness of Raphael's design for St Peter's with a drummed dome flanked by two towers with spires. It was in the Mantua collection acquired by Charles I, whose royal cipher, together with Vincenzo I Gonzaga's, is branded on the back of the panel. When the king's collection was sold by the Commonwealth, it was bought for £600 for Philip IV of Spain. It was looted by the French from the Sacristy of the Escorial during the Peninsular War. William Bankes was 'living in disguise' in Pamplona during the English siege in 1813 and dined with the French commanding officer 'who regaled him with a meal of rats washed down with strong drink'. To acquire

The Saloon with 'A Greate Landskip of Bergen's' and the Savonnerie carpet from Fonthill

the painting from his host he was obliged to purchase a donkey also and spent all his money apart from just enough for his passage home. He was 'peculiarly attached' to the donkey and presenting himself on board with the animal, the captain declared that 'the jackass should pay, like a gentleman'. He dined out on the story for years and had Princess Lieven in such uncontrollable laughter at the Duke of Wellington's table in February 1822, she left an account of it in her *Private Letters*. Forty years after sending home the painting Bankes commissioned the frame in 1853 from Pietro Giusti in Siena and modified the carver's design with the portrait medallions of the four previous owners. Giusti wrote that he had found medals in the Uffizi for the portraits of the Duke of Mantua, Charles I and Philip IV but that he would take Guidobaldo de Montefeltre, Duke of Urbino, from a painting of 1504. The frame was finished in time to be exhibited in Paris in 1855.

The *Four Elements: Air, Water, Earth, Fire*, from the studio of Jan Brueghel the Younger, are the latest paintings to enter the collection, acquired by the late Mr Bankes' father. The pair of superb young ladies of the Grimaldi family of Genoa by Rubens were acquired in 1840, according to William Bankes' own *ms* notes in two

Marchesa Caterina Grimaldi by Rubens

Marchesa Maria Grimaldi

editions of Ratti's *Guide to Genoa* in the Library. On the left is Marchesa Caterina Grimaldi in her wedding dress – she married Gian Vincenzo Imperiale in 1606 – and the portrait bears the date and signature of Rubens with the touching inscription '*Pinxit atque singulari devotiŏe*'. Marchesa Maria Grimaldi, her sister, is on the right with her dwarf and pet dog, whose collar bears the letters *M.A.* Another sitter, Marchesa Brigida Spinola, is now in the National Gallery in Washington. In these portraits Rubens, as a young man of twenty-nine, having made a profound study of Raphael, Titian and Tintoretto, has produced images of grandeur hardly to be surpassed.

The noble patrician whose portrait hangs above the chimneypiece was painted by Titian in the early 1540s. The sitter is probably Francesco Savorgnan della Torre, who died in 1547, rather than the military commander Girolamo who died in 1529. The del Torre branch of the Savorgnan family died out in 1810 when their collection was dispersed and their Venetian palace sold. According to William Bankes, the portrait was bought 'from the choice collection of the Avvocato Galeazzi' together with the *Judgement of Solomon* and two other unidentified pictures for 10,000 francs by Count Marescalchi, from whose palace in Bologna he purchased both masterpieces in 1820. Waagen saw the painting exhibited in London in 1856 and pronounced it 'very elevated in conception', but it was not at Kingston Lacy the following year when he visited the house.

The Spanish Room is on the left, but visitors are advised to complete the circuit of the Saloon first, re-passing the chimneypiece wall.

The only portrait of William Bankes himself, apart from Sandars' miniature of 1812 in the Drawing Room showcase, is the oil sketch by Sir George Hayter for the huge painting in the National Portrait Gallery of all the members who sat in the first Reform Parliament in 1833. The sketch stands on the inlaid table facing the windows, and is one of many the artist sold to his sitters when the large canvas was complete. William Bankes also sat later to Baron Marochetti who completed in the 1850s the plaster cast for a bronze or marble bust, never decided upon.

From the windows the park spreads out on the north side. Across the Saloon through the double doors the perspective leads into the Drawing Room and beyond the lawns on the south to William's obelisk.

On the east wall hang three large canvases, Richard Weston, 1st Earl of Portland, as Lord High Treasurer an unpopular but able financial agent for Charles I, from the studio of Van Dyck; the large Italianate landscape by Berchem, in Sir Ralph's possession before he built Kingston Hall, and the curious moralizing portrait of Edward Altham as a hermit. Altham was in Rome and Naples with his cousin, Jerome Bankes, in the 1650s, but the picture is thought to have been painted by Salvator Rosa about 1665. Supposed to have been a painter and pupil of Salvator Rosa, he is shown trampling on the works of Epicurus (no pleasure after death), regarding a skull and the gospels (the highest pleasure after death), while time is devouring strength in the shape of the Belvedere Torso on the relief (copied from Francois Perrier's *One Hundred Statues Spared by the Envious Tooth of Time*, 1638). William Bankes wrote in his notebook 'alter all the library frames and Lord Portland and Mr Altham to correspond with Charles and his Queen and Sir J. and Lady Borlase' – who retain their original Sunderland frames. Above the Berchem the *Omnia Vanitas* in the manner of Titian, previously in the Widmann collection, is another painting acquired in Bologna in 1820 from the Marescalchi palace and is described as *Venere Drajata del Tiziano* in the same document as the Savorgnan portrait.

Furniture

We know little of how the Saloon, or indeed the rest of the house, was furnished in Henry Bankes' time as no probate inventory has come to light for 1834. His son William, however, was offering the 'shallow bookcases made by my father for the Saloon' round the family in 1844 as they 'cannot accord in character with anything at Kingston Lacy'. A bill for two ebony chairs (there are six in the Entrance Hall) from Emanuel Brothers of Bishopsgate in 1838 (£12.3.6) shows that Bankes was acquiring the ebony seat furniture about this time, which entirely furnished the Saloon walls by 1856 in addition to the present scroll settees which were in the middle of the room. Such Anglo-Indian ebony furniture appealed to William Beckford, as can be seen in John Britton's *Illustrations of Fonthill Abbey*. The recluse's gothick lair was familiar to William Bankes from the youthful escapade he records in 1811, a year before he embarked on his wider and wilder eastern adventures, when he scaled the walls dressed as a workman, slipped through the front door, enjoyed a brief and furtive private view before narrowly avoiding confrontation with the owner who drove up as he was leaving among a band of navvies. Alas they did not meet, for fate was to deal the younger man a similar fall from social brilliance to ostracism for breaching sexual convention.

Twelve years later his father, Henry, listed half a dozen lots in the 1823 Fonthill sale in which he was interested and the auctioneer, Mr Phillips, wrote from the Abbey in September, asking 'to know *your Ideas* as to the Price of every lot you may wish for' – including the armchairs which he says in his subsequent letter in November '... averaged 15 gns *each chair*, which was considerably above your commission and consequently did not purchase them'. George Lucy of Charlecote in Warwickshire was more fortunate, acquiring much ebony furniture, lacquer and ceramics as well as the great *pietra dura* table from the Borghese Palace. Henry only succeeded in purchasing one object – lot 1546 – which he asked Mr Phillips to buy 'almost at any price': 'A *matchless* and MAGNIFICENT CARPET of the celebrated *Aubusson Factory*, of beautiful and rich antique pattern – this splendid object was manufactured expressly for the chateau at St Cloud in 1814, previous to the Abdication of Buonaparte'. He pencilled the measurements $(25' \times 24')$ into his copy of the sale catalogue in the Library at Kingston Lacy which, together with the plate of the grand drawing room in John

Rutter's *Delineations of Fonthill and its Abbey*, confirm that this is the carpet still in the Saloon. It is not an Aubusson but a Savonnerie and is of finer quality than those in the Drawing Room and the State Bedroom.

In December 1791 Frances Bankes, Henry's wife, wrote to her mother-in-law Margaret Wynne, who lived in Duke Street, Westminster, describing the ball they gave after Brettingham's alterations to the house were complete, '. . . The Ball Room was really very handsome, it was always a delightful room and I believe you saw enough of the Ceiling not to think I exaggerate when I say it looked beautiful, there is a noble lustre in the middle, and the Cornishes of the window Curtains are very large White and Gold with painted Medallions in them . . .'. Their lion-headed shield medallions are echoed in the painted ceiling. The 'noble lustre' is still here and was probably purchased new by them in the 1780s. 'The cornices from the London library had better go also [to Kingston Lacy] to resume their original place, they were only brought up to be out of the way of the dirt of the alterations, for they are in the best taste of anything that my father did in the way of fitting up', wrote her son William more than fifty years later in 1844.

Apart from the chandelier, the carpet and the window pelmets surviving from Henry and Frances Bankes' time, the rest of the furniture is mostly William's. The Anglo-Indian ebony settees are covered in the floral cross-stitch embroidery generally known as Berlin work but more correctly as overlaying work. The pair of eighteenth-century ebony caskets are also Indian, and the pair of Louis XIV *boulle* pedestals or *torchères*, rebuilt in the nineteenth century, are part of a set now widely dispersed, others being at Stratfield Saye, Uppark and in the Louvre. On them are a pair of canopic stands decorated with mummies and hieroglyphs in the *Retour d'Egypt* style, Paris, *c*.1805. The pair of walnut marquetry centre tables are nineteenth-century, made up with seventeenth-century cabinet doors for tops. Likewise, the Charles II box on its early nineteenth-century stand can be identified as the 'marquetrie Table made to your own top with new drawer, twisted pillars ebony and ivory bosses', supplied in June 1838 by Nixon and Son of Great Portland Street for £12. The *contre partie Boulle meuble d'entre deux*, built with eighteenth-century marquetry plaques, was in the London house in 1856 flanked by a pair of 4 foot cabinets forming a suite of three. The four *burgomeister* chairs are eighteenth-century Dutch or Portuguese colonial, three of satin-wood and one of ebony. In the marble niches at the south end of the Saloon stand a pair of Italian giltwood 'candelabra', a mermaid and a merman holding putti clasping cornucopia sprouting ormolu flowers for lights. William Bankes applied the tortoise-shell veneer to their triangular plinths, added the tortoises for feet and regilded them. The blue-ground *cloisonné* vases on the chimneypiece are eighteenth-century Chinese.

Sculpture and Carving

Bankes sent his sketches for the niches to Barry who gave the idea his blessing in January 1840, reducing their scale on the drawing and proposing 'the bead and enrichments . . . for the purpose of preventing the head of the niche from appearing dry and poor. This expedient you may remember is resorted to in some circular heads of Doorways in Florence particularly in the church of Santo Spirito, and in my opinion with good effect'. Barry was aware that his client liked an antiquarian or art-historical precedent for the features he adopted. Bankes' notes and sketches suggest his idea was based on shell niches in Montpellier and Narbonne, yet he later wrote '. . . you have a little model in wood of the shell at Milan from whence these were copied, where you can see how it was intended to be'. The shells were carved in yellow Torre marble by Michelangelo Montrésor in Verona in November 1847 and were shipped with the carved *Biancone* pilasters 'after two years of continued labour'. However, no Italian marble was of a colour quite suited to the back of the niche itself, and he tried in vain to obtain the green and white marble called *Campana* from Monsieur Geruset in Bordeaux. Finally in August 1854 he instructed Seymour to 'open therefore the two great cases (which you showed me) containing blocks of purple and white marble. . . . The quality of that marble being very rare and precious, it must be used with the least waste possible, that much may remain over for the capping of the Dining room dado'. This not only indicates something of his unrealized intentions for the decorations of the Dining Room, but suggests that perhaps he did make a visit to Kingston Lacy to supervise the works sometime between 1841 and 1854. This beautiful marble, so carefully and lovingly cut and carved by Seymour on William Bankes' minutest instructions, is called *Mischio di Seravezza* or sometimes *fleur de pêche*.

According to family tradition, the large pair of oak doors between the Saloon and the Drawing Room was acquired by William Bankes from the Vatican, for the arms of the Farnese Pope Paul III include the *fleur de lys*, 'the same as ours'. Bankes was a great collector of carved woodwork, which he then had made up into architectural and decorative features, but the carving, like the gilt dado rail, is eighteenth-century French. He complained of the 'gross folly of passing oil paint over that finely carved oak capping, which was not only primed for gilding but was actually gilt and required nothing but retouching here and there; let the gilder examine this and see what can be done' – but it was not remedied until 1985. Writing again in a critical mood from Lucca in May 1844 he says 'It is cruel too to have spoiled that glorious pair of doors between the two great rooms by putting the handles in the wrong place, and where no handles ever are in Italian doors, and of all things in the world, oak knobs in a room where there is gilding!! . . .'

Leave the doors to the staircase on your left and continue clockwise round the Saloon to reach the Spanish Room, re-entering the Drawing Room by the large double doors en route:

Miniatures

The large miniature on the second inlaid table, a watercolour on ivory by Sir William Ross, portrays Georgina Nugent, wife of George Bankes and sister-in-law to William, together with her three elder children in 1830. She left it to her youngest son Albert Bankes of Wolfeton, from whom it was bought by the late Mr Bankes' mother in 1906.

On re-entering the Drawing Room there is a closer view of Sir John and Lady Borlase by Van Dyck, some of the Bone enamels, including Sir John and Lady Bankes below the latter and Queen Elizabeth on the right of the chimneypiece. Above the Queen is the watercolour of the donor's mother painted in 1902 by Mary Gow. The small showcase contains the IOU from King Charles I for £525 for twenty horses supplied to him and a small plan of Corfe Castle drawn by Ralph Treswell in 1585. The miniature by Sandars of William Bankes in 1812 shows him as a young man of twenty-six about to set off on his travels in Spain. Once, there was also a miniature of Byron by the same artist after he came down from Trinity and just before he went abroad in 1809, which the poet gave to the Countess Albrizzi in Venice in 1819 or 1820 and was bought by William from her son in 1848. It has been replaced by an engraving. William Bankes also records that Hobhouse gave him a seal and a lock of Byron's hair.

Continue round the Saloon via the chimneypiece wall to the Spanish Room on the left.

The Spanish Room

If William Bankes sought to leave his own monument for posterity it is here in the 'Golden Room' or 'Spanish Picture Room' as he called it. He created it between 1838 and 1855 with consummate success as the rich and sombre, completely harmonious setting for the Spanish paintings acquired in his youth nearly forty years before.

Originally the bedchamber to the anteroom or great hall on Pratt's plan, with adjoining closets as on the other corners of the house, it became the eating room in the 1780s when Brettingham brought the great dining room, or great chamber above the present Drawing Room, downstairs for Henry Bankes. This proved incommodiously small, and among the drawings for schemes to enlarge the room are those by Thomas Cundy (1820) and by Jeffrey Wyatt (1821). All were rejected on grounds of cost until, in 1833, a block-like single bay was extended to the west, only to be demolished promptly after Henry's death when William adopted Barry's solution in the present Dining Room. The huge brick arch of the extended eating room came to light on the west wall in 1983 when the leather hangings were removed for restoration.

William Bankes' early enthusiasm for collecting Spanish pictures encouraged him to send home more geese than swans, yet the thought and care he lavished on their arrangement and setting over many years resulted in an ensemble of some beauty, constituting an original contribution to mid nineteenth-century taste. As always, his evolving ideas are documented in great, sometimes confusing, detail with his memoranda, sketches, specifications and designs for the decorations.

The Ceiling

He purchased the Venetian ceiling on the London market and adapted it to the Spanish Picture Room in 1838. He paid Town and Emanuel of 103 New Bond Street £100 for 'a Venetian Ceiling' in March 1839. This was soon after the contents of the Palazzo Contarini degli Scrigni were dispersed and William Bankes wrote an account 'of the Contarini ceiling. This ceiling had been purchased on speculation by some Jews in London, upon the faith of a very beautiful and accurate drawing sent over to them from Venice, which is now in my possession . . . In the fitting, some modifications were required to make the dimensions conform for the original figures [measurements] had more of a gallery-proportion, falling short in the breadth by a very few inches but exceeding the length included within the present walls by several feet.' The breadth he increased by adding 'a narrow margin or styling, slightly sunk in cavetto . . . between the outermost moulded framing of the ceiling and the cymatum of the en- tablature: on the other hand what in the length was more than sufficient, was retrenched by the simple omission of two pieces of flourished work in relief', which in any case 'partook of that fantastic and licentious taste' out of keeping with the rest of the design which he attributed to Sansovino. Although the room has not yet been identified, the ceiling may be from one of those 'of gallery-proportion' in the Palazzo Contarini degli Scrigni, with its two *piani nobili*, which Scamozzi added to the old Palazzo Contarini Corfu on the Grand Canal in 1609. The detailed fitting of the ceiling to the old eating room proportions was confirmed by the different kinds of gilding observed by the conservators who worked on the ceiling in 1984.

The oval cartouches in the frieze, whether or not from the same room, Bankes in- scribed as labels for the paintings below (the space between them and the shells was to be filled with 'gilded cords and tassels'), adding in 1854 the metal ropework originally intended for the tapestry-hung Saloon. The cartouches had evidently been badly stored for some time, for in 1854 he sent instructions to take them out and put them in safety, and 'try whether bread will not clean away the coal dust' on 'that unlucky cartouche which was found in the coal hole'.

The Leather

The leather skins were difficult to collect in sufficient quantity and in the end some new ones were ordered to make up the total required. Venice had an assured supply of leather from a Black Sea port, and a number of palazzi on the Grand Canal once covered their walls in this manner, tapestries being less suitable for the humid climate. Little remains in Venice today, a notable example being the walls of the Palazzo Vendramin-Calergi, the original home of the *Judgement of Solomon* and now the muni- cipal winter casino. Bankes wrote from Venice in 1849 'I have at length purchased hangings of gilded leather sufficient, I trust, for the whole walls, but as the quantity runs very close, I want the utmost precision in the dimensions'. It cost him 'about

Drawing of
the Contarini
ceiling

13 shillings the square yard, without jointing or carriage' he calculated. He gave numbers of skins, and their exact dimensions, of 'embossed and gilded leather bought from the Palazzo Contarini (allo Scrigno)'. Most of it is not embossed like Dutch leather, but tooled and painted as in bookbinding. There were about 120 skins from the Contarini Palace exclusive of the border, 91 of one pattern and 31 of another. In July 1851 Antonio Caldero contracted to restore 'all the gilt leather taken from a palace in SS Apostoli, already the property of Mr Bankes' for 12 Austrian Lire per square metre (72 square metres=864 AL, noted Bankes). Another draft contract of April 1852 for 19 AL per square metre is to make all the gilded leather missing from this series. It was all shipped in the brig *Marcolo Polo* in January 1853, followed by very detailed dimensions, drawings and minute instructions for fitting and stretching it on battens 'because I consider the air at the back to be an advantage', reminiscent of those sent to his upholsterer by William Blathwayt of Dyrham Park one hundred and fifty years earlier.

A hundred and thirty years later the bad 'varnish consigned to the Captain' and light had rendered the leather a sorry sight and in need of drastic attention. Modern techniques of leather conservation can deal with the levels of acidity and animal fat by treatment of the back of the skins, but the visible surfaces were beyond recall. Happily, the Spanish paintings are large and the leather behind the canvases had been preserved from both light and more malicious varnish. After treatment in Holland, the conservators restitched all the skins to hide the damaged ones and display those hitherto protected, so restoring the room to its original glowing beauty.

The Doors

The three pairs of painted doors are best described by William Bankes in a letter to his sister, Lady Falmouth, from Venice on 14 June 1851 'They are a work which has been in hand upwards of three years, done entirely from my designs, and under my eye and direction, and in many parts touched by my own hand. The artist (who had no celebrity before) is thought to have done himself great credit, and had in consequence now as many orders as he can execute, and I see every reason to be satisfied with him. They bear and require minute examination from their extreme finish; being twelve in number, they represent the months of the year – six upon gold, as the summer months, and six upon bronze as the winter. With them are my original drawings for them, which will be deposited with you. These are sketchily painted in water colour, and dirtied in the process of copying, and blurred here and there with alterations, but they constitute, I believe, my best and certainly my largest work in drawing, and have at least the merit, such as it is, of being entirely of my own invention, so that they will have some interest at least for you.' These drawings for the twelve panels painted on pear wood with walnut styles and rails are still at Kingston Lacy.

He sent instructions for removing, staining and slowly drying the carvings on the sunk shutter panels, which were to have the ground painted red, the styling a deep

34

green and the beading gilded and burnished, 'always harmonising the gold with the ceiling'. The garlands of pendant fruit and flower swags were to receive 'a slight sprinkling of gold' after one was to be sent to him in France so that he could provide the sample treatment.

Sculpture and Picture Frames

The cabinet at the end of the room is faced with Florentine mosaic or *pietra dura* contracted for by the Buoninsegni brothers for 1125 *francesconi* on 28 October 1850, to be executed within two years from William Bankes' own designs, which were not to be used again and are still in the house. Two panels of pendant garlands either side of the chimneypiece are less well documented. In the 1930s Daphne Bankes wrote they were 'single blocks of marble from the Fabricotti quarries outside Florence – said to be the largest slabs ever found there – the natural veining very cleverly used by the artist for the fruits etc'. Bankes sent them over with very detailed instructions about how they were to be re-fitted into black marble from Ireland or Anglesey, 'as designed, none of superior quality being to be had in Toulouse'.

The unified scheme for the setting of his Spanish paintings was crowned by his concern for the harmonious gilding of the various elements, especially the three new

The Spanish Room

frames en suite for the centre paintings on each wall, as well as that in the centre of the ceiling. Giuseppe Foradori was paid 50 AL in advance in April 1848 for the third frame. Two are the frames on *Las Meninas* on the east wall and *St Augustine* over the chimneypiece. The third framed a portrait of Philip IV by Velasquez (acquired in June 1827 with the two large Snyders on the staircase from the Altamira collection) which hung in the middle of the west wall in 1856 but was sold in 1896 and is now in the Isabella Stewart Gardner Museum in Boston. The frames are nineteenth-century versions of a type known as a 'Sansovino' frame. Bankes wrote to his sister from Florence in November 1850 'I sent over three gloriously carved frames for the three centre pictures of that room which are now gilding in London'. To Osborne he wrote 'They are Venetian frames and I choose them to be done in the Venetian manner . . .' and he was to take samples of the reduced ceiling to the gilder so that they would match the gilding of the Contarini ceiling.

The other gilt frames in the Spanish Room with their composition shells or enriched corners, are of a kind used throughout the house, and were probably made in Henry Bankes' lifetime, about 1815–20, when his son's Spanish paintings were arriving at the house. William sketched an early scheme to hang them in what looks like the north parlour (now the State Bedroom) from the position of the doors.

Pictures

Visiting this 'very rich and tastefully adorned apartment' in 1857 the German art-historian Waagen wrote 'I know no other collection in England containing so many valuable pictures of the Spanish school'. The *Two Peasant Boys Eating Fruit* belonged to Sir Ralph Bankes in 1659 and was known to be a copy; the original is in the Alte Pinakothek in Munich. The other paintings were collected by William Bankes during his travels in Spain between 1812 and 1814, when the Peninsular War displaced many works of art. He describes them to his father Henry in his letters from Alicante in October 1814 and from Cairo in September 1815 'You . . . will . . . receive three cases of pictures that I left at Cadiz, which Sir John Louis promised to convey in *L'Aigle* frigate . . . I have several here [Alicante] three Murillos, one Velasquez, many Alonso Cano, which I have brought from convents in Granada and the interior – they will remain here probably a twelvemonth before being shipped off'. He is surprised that 'you do not think more highly of the Ribalta' as he 'had the opinions of several good judges before I bought it, for all the court was in Valencia at the time'. *Santa Justa,* one of the patron saints of Seville, probably belonged to a series of virgin saints, like *St Dorothy*, painted by Zurbaran's studio. He attributed *St Augustine* to Spagnoletto, saying it belonged to Philibert, Duke of Savoy, and came from the cathedral at Placencia. 'Do not have it cleaned till I come . . . I would not have it touched for the world.' 'I am not surprised that my Espinosa pleases you' – the Valencian nobleman's name was not to be lost, 'If you have had it stretched and mounted I beg the name and title may be written on the back'. The *Sleeping Child* was 'In the very best manner of Alonso Cano' but 'The Orrentes are not so good as I could have wished'. Juanes 'is the only considerable Spanish painter that is wanting' and he gave a place on his wall plan to an Assumption of the Virgin by that artist as he was 'still in treaty for it and hope in process of time to bring [the owner who was asking too much money] to reason'.

'The little Angel by Murillo was cut out by the French of one of his most famous pictures . . . in the Capuchin convent at Seville' and was found covering the knapsack of a dead French soldier. 'Sir Henry Wellesley has in his charge the glory of my collection, the Velasquez' . . . *Las Meninas* . . . 'I was a long while in treaty for it and was obliged at last to give a high price.' He was persuaded that it was the original sketch for the famous painting in the Prado of the maids of honour with their mistress the Infanta Margarita at the court of Philip IV, but it is an early and uninspiring copy. If the young William Bankes' judgement was enthusiastic but erratic, he was nevertheless, for an Englishman, ahead of his time in forming his Spanish collection.

By contrast, the sitter in the very fine portrait by Velasquez of *Cardinal Massimi*, which Bankes bought later in 1820 in Bologna, had long been forgotten and was only recognized in 1958. Camillo Massimi (1620–77), the connoisseur, patron and friend of Poussin and Claude as well as of Velasquez, was Papal Nuncio to Spain in 1654–58, when Velasquez wrote him a letter of welcome. He was painted by Velasquez in Rome during the artist's second visit to Italy in 1649–50, most unusually in the *habitato da prelato* – the official costume of a *cameriere segreto*, a personal appointment of the Pope, with the silk *sottana* and serge *soprana* in peacock blue painted in rare and costly ultramarine pigment which would have been hard to obtain in Spain. This was strikingly revealed by recent cleaning, when the cipher and inventory number of Don Gaspar de Haro, Marqués del Carpio was found on the back of the original canvas. This Spanish collector and patron of Velasquez was Ambassador to the Holy See at the time he acquired the portrait on the sitter's death in 1677, then Viceroy in Naples from 1682 until he died there in 1687. No more is then known of 'the portrait of an ecclesiastic', until William Bankes purchased it in Bologna, later observing that it had 'a richer tone of colour than the generality of his works in Spain'.

Furniture

Henry Bankes purchased the Axminster carpet from Samuel Whitty around 1820. The four chairs carved in the style of Daniel Marot are nineteenth-century. The eight-day striking mantel clock is signed by Francis Raynsford (*c.*1667–after 1704), a 'watch maker at Charing Cross', but was in fact made by Edward Appley (*c.*1656–88) about 1688. The clock was probably part of his stock passed on to Raynsford who was in business after 1688. The pier-glasses between the windows are Queen Anne, rebuilt and regilded for the room. The 'Spanish gypsy cauldrons', the George III-style dining chairs and the gilt cabinet were bought by the late Mr Bankes' father. In the gilt cabinet are a series of four early seventeenth-century gilt bronze plaques depicting

Apollo and Python, Mercury and Endymion, Apollo and Daphne, and Mercury and Argus; and a group of drawings and miniatures cut out from large manuscripts. Two of these were in Sir Ralph Bankes' possession in 1659 – 'A Peice of Water Coulors of Pilates Judgement of our Saviour' and 'Another Peice of Water Coulors of our Saviour att Supper'. The first is in the style of Simon Bening after Schongauer about 1525, while the second is of the school of the Loire or of Bourdichon about 1500.

Returning via the Saloon the marble staircase is reached by the doors to the left of the marble niche. Turn left into the State Bedroom.

The State Bedroom

In Pratt's layout of the 1660s this was the little parlour with a corner closet and small staircase to the basement, echoing the arrangement of at least one of the other three corner apartments on the principal floor. It must have been opened up by Brettingham in the 1780s to make the north parlour or Frances Bankes could not have sat so many people at supper for her ball in 1791. Barry subdivided it again in the 1830s but the walnut cornice is eighteenth century. The ceiling was probably made by Costante Traversi in the early 1850s – 'an old carved ceiling to be reduced' is mentioned as being in the hands of the artist in 1855. In May 1855, after William Bankes died, Traversi records 'Two ceilings in the Lombard style were commissioned by Mr W. Bankes' from him and all the work was in hand and would cost 3440 Austrian Lire when complete in eight months' time. The British Consul in Venice suspended work on the ceilings and that for the Library had been abandoned to please Lady Falmouth anyway, but the State Bedroom ceiling was later carried out as indicated on Seymour's drawings by Bankes six months before his death. 'Do nothing that can by possibility disturb Lady Falmouth who sleeps in the room over' he wrote. The paintings in the ceiling, attributed by Bankes to Veronese and Padovanino, are part of a larger ceiling that included the octagonal painting now over the Staircase, which he bought in 1849 from the sixteenth-century Grimani palace at Santa Maria Formosa built by the Patriarch of Aquileia. 'Nothing but the distress produced by the siege of Venice could have brought it within a sum that I was willing to give', he wrote in 1850, '. . . since nobody had a farthing, and anything might be had for money.'

Furniture

The bed was also unfinished at William Bankes' death in 1855, when Mr Malcolm's correspondence with his brother George reveals his reluctance in settling William's affairs – 'It is a great inconvenience to me to have to look after all these artists, and it is quite impossible for me to dedicate sufficient time to superintend the proper carrying out and finishing these works of Art'. The 'state bedstead' is carved in holly and the carver is probably Vincenzo Favenza, for he was protesting vigorously in

October 1855 to the Bankes heirs demanding compensation for taking away his commission. Some of the carved reliefs derive from antique gems and drawings; for example the central group of cupids from a gem now in Boston, engraved by Bartolozzi after G.C.B. Cipriani; the Jupiter and Juno from a study by Annibale Carracci for a fresco in the Galleria Farnese of about 1600. Among the other carved features are the Bankes coat of arms and the bats. Mr Malcolm wrote to George Bankes in August 1855 '. . . I cannot but say that if it is carried out as intended it would be throwing away money and I believe your brother was fully aware of the mistake in design and taste,' and in the following October 'The only thing of any importance on hand which is not in a forward state is the Bed; I have been trying to stop this, as your son wrote to me such to be your desire, at first the party had exhorbitant ideas, but I have brought him to reduce his demand to 100 Napoleons, about £80 – to give all up as it is, and renounce all claims, my candid opinion is that you had better thus get rid of it, have it all packed up and sent off; but you must just do in this as you may judge best'. It had not arrived by 1860 when the inventory made on the death of George's son, Edmund George Bankes, still refers to this room as the 'North Parlour'.

The Kaiser's visit in 1908

The room is now essentially a private one rather than for the display of works of art. The wallpaper is a Christopher Dresser design of the 1890s. A garniture of three Delftware blue and white baluster vases c.1690, possibly acquired by John Bankes the Elder, stand on the Dutch walnut seaweed marquetry cabinet-on-stand (Jan Roohals and I. Hoogeboom have inscribed their names within). Above hangs a nineteenth-century Windsor tapestry of Europa and the Bull purchased by W.R.Bankes. There are group photographs of the Kaiser's visit to Kingston Lacy in 1907 and that of the Princess of Wales in 1908; and of the late Ralph Bankes in naval uniform.

Beyond is the Bathroom (State Dressing Room) with a ceiling modelled on one at the Queen's House, Greenwich. William Bankes wished the 'parquet floor for the Dressing Room to correspond in pattern with the compartments of the ceiling'.

The Upper Marble Staircase

Sculpture

The third flight rises centrally within the well of the staircase and turns at the next landing by a copy of a Roman marble candelabrum. The lizard on the plinth below is the work of a carver called Moro who worked for Michelangelo Montrésor in Verona. The two bronze busts of Sir John Bankes stand on Italian baroque pedestals carved with fauns, either side of 'one of the white wooden pedestals which were always in the house, for a light or a bust' intended by William Bankes for this position, on which is a plaster bust of William Pitt the Younger, the friend of Henry Bankes. Under the windows are copies of the sculpted frieze known as *The Borghese Dancers* in the Louvre and its pendant showing maidens adorning a candelabrum. The longer relief of dancing putti was commissioned by William Bankes from one of his Italian craftsmen and is copied from works by Della Robbia and Donatello. The garlands of birds and of fishes inset in the pilasters of the staircase are inscribed and dated 1846 and were carved by Salesio Angelo Pegrassi from William Bankes' own designs. The top landing has three domes decorated with wreaths of bay and ribbons and the balustrade is of alabaster capped with *Biancone*. 'The two Candelabra in Biancone to stand on the capping of the long top landing of the marble stairs are just about to be sent home in a schooner called the Stamboul' wrote William Bankes in April 1854 and they were carved from his own sketch. The four bronze figures resting on green serpentine plinths are small versions of Michelangelo's monumental *Times of Day* in the Medici Chapel in Florence.

Pictures

The two large canvases by Frans Snyders were bought from the Altamira collection in 1827. They had been looted by Napoleon in Madrid and sent to the Gobelins for tapestries to be made but were returned to the owner after 1815, who subsequently sold them in London. These large canvases are framed by plaster swags of flowers and fruit, presumably rearranged when the paintings were moved here from the Dining Room in the 1890s. Barry's ceiling, like that in the Dining Room, is inspired by Pratt's work at Coleshill and in the centre is a *trompe l'oeil* painting with putti disporting in a cupola of vine trellis. This was thought by William Bankes to be the work of Giorgione and was part of the large ceiling he acquired in 1849 during the siege of Venice from the Grimani palace at Santa Maria Formosa.

Furniture

Below the painting of the horse attacked by wolves, is 'a very fine Venetian table' bought from John Webb of 8 Old Bond Street in June 1839 for £20. The William and

The Upper Marble Staircase

Mary marquetry longcase clock is by Francis Raynsford (see page 37), and the Charles II lacquer cabinet on a giltwood stand might be one of the pieces purchased in the 1690s by John and Margaret Bankes.

In due course the two bedroom suites will be restored. Meanwhile in the White Bedroom on the right an exhibition has been arranged with models to show the architectural history of the house and the work of the three main architects, Sir Roger Pratt, Robert Furze Brettingham and Sir Charles Barry. Here is Pratt's original drawing for the entrance elevation on the north, and Pratt's structure can be seen exposed showing the recent repairs in steel.

The South-east Bedroom, Cabinet Room and Dressing Room

The worsted Brussels carpet has been rewoven from a fragment dating from before 1850 that was found in another bedroom in the house. Opposite the windows are two portraits of John Bankes the Younger painted in 1733 and in 1764, and on his right is his brother Henry Bankes the Elder. On the right of the bed the two small ovals are of the same John Bankes as a small boy and his father John Bankes the Elder, both painted in 1702. The portraits in the brown frames are of the Parker family; Margaret Parker, on the right of Zoffany's conversation piece, married John Bankes the Elder. In the centre of the *Woodley Family* painted by Zoffany is Frances Woodley, whose full-length portrait by Romney is in the Drawing Room, and one of the other little girls is her sister Maria, Mrs Riddell. The set of four mahogany serpentine chests of drawers here and in the Dressing Room may be by Ince and Mayhew, but a bill has not been found. The painted oval pier-glass is *c*.1770.

The small Cabinet Room next door has one of Barry's coved and decorated plaster ceilings. The fine eighteenth-century cabinet and stand of padouk wood inlaid with ivory is Anglo-Indian (Vizagapatam). The chalk drawing is a rare portrait of the actor Thomas Betterton in the part of Bajazet in Marlowe's *Tamburlaine the Great*. On the far wall are six small enamel miniatures by Henry Bone (see page 17).

Over the Dressing Room chimneypiece is a pastel portrait of Walter Ralph Bankes (1853–1904) by Laura Hope, and on the opposite wall prints and photographs of William's brother George Bankes (1787–1856) and three of his sons, Edmund George Bankes, Henry Hyde Nugent Bankes and Albert Bankes of Wolfeton House, Dorchester, who was a frequent guest at Kingston Lacy when he helped the late Mr Bankes' widowed mother to entertain; also portraits of Ralph Bankes and his sisters. Opposite the window is a portrait of Dr John Wynne, Bishop of Bath and Wells, whose Welsh property descended to William Bankes through his grandmother; portrait prints of the Duke of Wellington and Byron; and a pair of watercolours of Corfe Castle.

The Bedroom Corridor and Attic Staircase

The Corridor, with its barrel vault and coffered ceiling, is part of Brettingham's alterations of the 1780s. The first portrait on the left is of Mary Luttrell, Lady Rooke, bought by John Bankes for two guineas in 1738. At the end of the Corridor is Barry's ingenious apse leading to bathrooms and bedrooms and lit by carefully contrived natural light from the alabaster shells and fanlights. At the top of the stairs are three carved panels which could possibly be part of Pratt's original house, but equally they may have been acquired by William Bankes in the 1830s. Beyond is Barry's six-sided cupola with its frieze of baroque swags of fruit suspended from lion masks and either side of the lantern are two plaster wreaths of fruit decorated with ribbons. The attic passages are hung with the store collection of pictures, including the large painting of the *Circumcision* after a Dürer woodcut.

Visitors descend right to the bottom of the staircase and turn left before the great fireplace in the Hall to leave the house by the Back Hall and the Servants' Hall.

The Servants' Hall and the Kitchen Courtyard

In the Back Hall is the well-stocked butler's silver cupboard and some fine eighteenth-century dress swords by the best London and Paris sword makers including Robert Gray, James Cullum, James Shrapnell and Lecourt. In the Servants' Hall hangs a group of paintings collected in the seventeenth or early eighteenth century, Dutch landscapes and primitive *capricci* of Roman ruins in their original black frames, demoted from the state rooms in the early nineteenth century by William Bankes' fresh acquisitions. The adjacent room, formerly the housekeeper's room and then the Billiard Room since 1930, will be arranged to display William Bankes' Egyptian collection as soon as funds permit.

The eighteenth-century Kitchen Courtyard was designed by W. Rice, Surveyor to HM Customs, for Henry Bankes the Elder in 1775–76, with the laundry and drying room on the south (left-hand) side. The north range was enlarged in the 1780s by Brettingham for his son Henry's kitchen, which now contains the shop. The sculleries and store rooms have been thrown together to make an exhibition room. Beyond lies the stable range of 1882 where the tea room has been installed.

Turn left before the stables for the garden.

The Garden and the Park

Sculpture on the Terrace

Barry added the Terrace, modelled on the Queen's House at Greenwich, for William Bankes who purchased the 'pair of bronze vases with cupid handles from Versailles' in 1841 for 68 guineas (lot 213, Christie's, 30 April). Several Paris bronze founders made copies of the thirteen different original designs at Versailles but this pair predate the 46 ordered by Lord Hertford for the Bagatelle in 1854, some of which are now at Sissinghurst, Lanhydrock and the Wallace Collection. The ten bronze 'vases' on the balustrade are sockets for the poles which supported a striped awning slung from the bronze rings above and they came from Marochetti's workshop. Bankes commissioned the two lions in *rosso Veronese*, copied in smaller scale from those at the foot of the Capitol in Rome, from the sculptor Petrelli in January 1848. The eight Carrara vases or '*tazzas*' were ordered from Micali of Leghorn in November 1852 and the bronze lions were cast by Comperot. 'Think of my carrying a live Tortoise in a bag all the way from the Palais Royal!' wrote William from Paris to his sister in October 1853 'when you see it multiplied to the number of sixteen' by Marochetti to support the four Verona 'upright vases' at each end of the gravel path. The late Mr Bankes' mother added more of the marble vases and the marble seat in 1911, with another pair of bronze vases in 1912.

The Garden

On the left is the 'Dutch Garden' laid out in 1899 by C. E. Ponting, the Salisbury diocesan architect who designed the church at Pamphill in 1907 for Mrs Bankes in memory of her husband. These beds are now planted in her seasonal schemes of pink begonias or wallflowers. William Goldring of Kew was consulted for planting schemes from 1899 to 1906. Mrs Bankes' garden in its heyday between the wars has been recorded by Mr Edward Dukes the retired head gardener.

On the right is the Victorian fernery, restored by the Trust, leading to the Cedar Walk with one of the Duke of Wellington's cedars planted in 1827 and commemorative trees planted from 1905 to 1935 by visiting royalty and members of the family. The path turns left at the sundial down the ancient Lime Avenue to Nursery Wood, with a collection of trees, and Spoon Walk planted with flowering shrubs, whence the visitor can return to the house via the Cedar Avenue planted by William in 1835.

The Wellheads on the Lawn

The six wellheads or 'marble tubs' for bay trees are the work of William and his carvers in Verona from 1847 to 1851. Two are old ones from the courtyards of 'Palazzo la Bernardo' and 'Palazzo Breganza' in Venice, where a substitute had to be provided for the former. One of the red marble ones was 'copied at Verona full size from one in the court of a palace of the Bevilacqua family' by the Montrésor workshop. Another 'on which I have endeavoured to represent by boys the four seasons . . . is my most considerable design in figures' and was carved in Istrian marble by Giordani. In 1853 William specified deal box covers to protect the sculpture in winter and Kingston Lacy is one of the few places where this practice, now being followed everywhere in the Trust's gardens, has continued uninterrupted, though the boxes were painted white and not green as he wished. George Evamy, a retired gardener writing in the last century, described a wood cover for the obelisk, 'but it was let run to decay'.

The Obelisk

William Bankes first saw his pink granite obelisk in 1815. It is the eastern of a pair raised in front of the temple of Isis on the island of Philae, now inundated. It bears the names of Ptolemy VII Euergetes II who died in 116 BC, and his second consort Cleopatra III and records the exemption granted to the priests of Isis from bearing the expenses of the local administration, which, according to their petition, were ruining the temple. William entrusted its removal to the ex-music hall giant and engineer Belzoni. After 'descending majestically into the river' and causing a skirmish with the French, it arrived in England in 1821. The Duke of Wellington saw it in the docks and was enthusiastic about it, offering to send it down to Dorset on a gun carriage. He came to Kingston Lacy to lay the foundation stone in April 1827. Linant de Bellefonds sent the remaining fragment of the companion obelisk and the three huge steps of granite from Maharraga to form the platform in 1829, when it was finally erected. It had been damaged in transit on its long journey and was repaired with granite from the ruins of Leptis Magna given by King George III.

William had published the *Geometrical elevations of an Obelisk . . . from the Island of Philae, together with the pedestal . . . first discovered there by W. J. Bankes* with the hieroglyphs and Greek inscriptions in 1821, offering a brilliant suggestion which brought the obelisk into the climax of the somewhat acrimonious debate on the hieroglyphic problem, which was finally unravelled by Champollion.

His father, Henry Bankes, wrote to his daughter-in-law Georgina in August 1829 that 'the bricks are deposited opposite my window for the foundation of William's Obelisk, and the granite steps are actually in Pool, but not yet out of the vessel. I wish that he had placed the whole at Soughton, where there is a small walled court before his principal front, much better adapted to it than my spacious lawn: but I submit to it as a disorder in the Bankes family, which sometimes passes over one

The Philae Obelisk

generation, like madness or gout, or the king's evil, and breaks out again in the next: my uncle . . . could not help erecting two Obelisks; and thought he had done enough.' These eighteenth-century obelisks are shown on the plan of the garden and park in the estate survey made after his brother's death for Henry Bankes the Elder in 1773–74 by William Woodward and they were then framed by diagonal avenues in the park. One still survives there on the south-west but W. R. Bankes replaced the other in 1887 with a new one nearby to commemorate Queen Victoria's Jubilee. It is reached by taking the path called Blind Walk.

The original owner of the sarcophagus was Amenemopet, chief steward of Amun in Thebes during the Reign of Rameses I (1313–1292 BC) and his tomb is at Luxor. Henry Salt the British consul gave it to William and wrote in January 1822 hoping it would 'form an acceptable addition to your Egyptian antiquities'.

The Park

In the 1770s the Park and adjacent enclosed field was of about 210 acres. Its present shape and size of 399 acres is due to Henry Bankes the Younger who landscaped it, doing away with the formal avenues, and extended it after the Enclosure Act of 1784, when the line of the Turnpike Road was moved further to the north. He only spared the existing Lime Avenue which is the sole survivor of the original layout shown in Woodward's survey. He planted 2,000 beech trees in the woodland belt on the new boundaries. Its present aspect, however, dotted rather than clumped with mature trees, reflects successive plantings in the nineteenth century. William Bankes planted the great beech avenue stretching for two and a half miles towards Blandford in 1835 and the oak avenue on Pamphill Green in 1842, according to George Evamy the old gardener.

Bankes Family Tree abridged to show **owners** of Kingston Lacy and Portraits* in the house

M = Miniature   **P** = Photograph, print or drawing

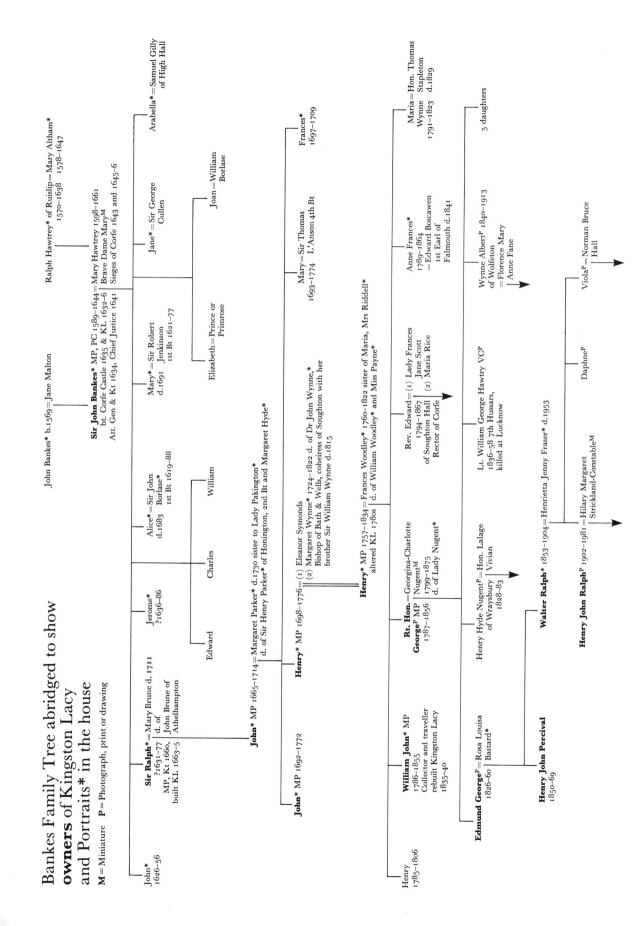

John Bankes* b.1569 = Jane Malton

Ralph Hawtrey* of Ruislip = Mary Altham*
1570–1638   1578–1647

Sir John Bankes* MP, PC 1589–1644 = Mary Hawtrey 1598–1661
bt. Corfe Castle 1635 & KL 1632–6   Brave Dame Mary M
Att. Gen & Kt 1634, Chief Justice 1641   Sieges of Corfe 1643 and 1645–6

John* 1626–56

Jane = Sir George Cullen

Arabella = Samuel Gilly of High Hall

Joan = William Borlase

Sir Ralph* = Mary Brune d.1711
?1631–77   d. of John Brune of
MP, Kt 1660,   Athelhampton
built KL 1663–5

Jerome* ?1636–86

Alice* = Sir John Borlase*
d.1683   1st Bt 1619–88

William

Mary* = Sir Robert Jenkinson
d.1691   1st Bt 1621–77

Elizabeth = Prince or Primrose

Mary = Sir Thomas L'Anson 4th Bt
1693–1774

Frances*
1697–1709

Edward   Charles

John* MP 1665–1714 = Margaret Parker* d.1730 sister to Lady Pakington*
d. of Sir Henry Parker* of Honington, 2nd Bt and Margaret Hyde*

Henry* MP 1698–1776 == (1) Eleanor Symonds
(2) Margaret Wynne* 1724–1822 d. of Dr John Wynne,*
Bishop of Bath & Wells, coheiress of Soughton with her
brother Sir William Wynne d.1815

John* MP 1692–1772

Henry* MP 1757–1834 = Frances Woodley* 1760–1822 sister of Maria, Mrs Riddell*
altered KL 1780s   d. of William Woodley* and Miss Payne*

Henry 1785–1806

William John* MP
1786–1855
Collector and traveller
rebuilt Kingston Lacy
1835–40

**Rt. Hon.
George*** MP
1787–1856
= Georgina-Charlotte Nugent M
1799–1875
d. of Lady Nugent*

Rev. Edward = (1) Lady Frances Jane Scott
1794–1867   (2) Maria Rice
of Soughton Hall
Rector of Corfe

Maria = Hon. Thomas Wynne Stapleton
1791–1823   d.1829

Anne Frances*
1789–1864
= Edward Boscawen
1st Earl of
Falmouth d.1841

Edmund George P = Rosa Louisa
1826–60   Bastard*

Henry Hyde Nugent* P = Hon. Lalage
of Wraysbury   Vivian
1828–83

Lt. William George Hawtry VC P
1836–58 7th Hussars,
killed at Lucknow

Wynne Albert* P 1840–1913
of Wolfeton
= Florence Mary
Anne Fane

5 daughters

Henry John Percival
1850–69

Walter Ralph* 1853–1904 = Henrietta Jenny Fraser* d.1953

Viola* P = Norman Bruce Hall

Henry John Ralph P 1902–1981 = Hilary Margaret
Strickland-Constable M

Daphne* P

The Bankes Family of Kingston Lacy and Corfe Castle

Sir John Bankes (1589–1644) came from an old yeoman family in Cumberland, went up to Oxford and then to Gray's Inn, was called to the bar in 1614 and married Mary Hawtrey in 1618. He entered Parliament in the 1620s, when he also acquired an interest in the black lead or graphite mine in Borrowdale. He became Attorney-General in 1634 and was knighted, it being said at the time 'that he exceeds Bacon in eloquence, Chancellor Ellesmere in judgement and William Noy in law'. By 1636 he had purchased his two estates in Dorset. He was promoted to Chief Justice of the Common Pleas in 1641. He was always deeply loyal to his monarch but his caution and moderation led him into the role of mediator between King and Parliament at a critical and momentous time. He died at Oxford in December 1644 where his monument on the wall of Christchurch Cathedral was carved by the sons of Nicholas Stone. His wife, Brave Dame Mary, withstood two sieges of Corfe Castle and lived to see the Restoration of the monarchy, but the castle was left in ruins.

Large sums were paid by Lady Bankes and her children to regain the family property and her sons travelled abroad during the Commonwealth. John, the eldest who died young (1626–56), and Ralph (?1631–77) signed the books they purchased in the late 1640s. Jerome and his cousin Edward Altham were in Rome in 1654 and both had their portraits painted in Italy. Three years after his elder brother died Ralph listed his pictures in 1659, the year he entered Parliament. He was living comfortably at Gray's Inn in an informed circle that included Lely. Knighted at the Restoration, he married Mary Brune of Athelhampton the following year and employed Roger Pratt to build the new family seat at Kingston Hall from 1663–65. He failed to recover either the materials taken from Corfe by Sir Walter Erle to build Charborough, or the furnishings of the castle appropriated by Colonel Bingham and Pratt's notes say nothing of how the house was furnished. He was, however, quite seriously in debt when he died in 1677 when he willed that his books and his pictures should be kept together for his son and not sold.

John Bankes (1665–1714) was a minor and the house was later let to the Duke of Ormonde who died here in 1688. John married Margaret Parker in 1691 and she records in her accounts how they furnished the house when they moved back to Kingston Hall. None of the rich furniture and fabrics survive, except perhaps one mirror, a japan cabinet and 'the china to sett on the cabinet' might be the Delftware garniture of three baluster vases of the 1690s. Their two sons, John (1692–1772) and Henry (1698–1776) were both interested in pictures. John had 128 paintings cleaned in 1738 and Henry made an inventory of them in 1762. John remained a bachelor, built up funds and added to the Bankes' estates. Henry, a barrister, took over his brother's seat in Parliament in 1741 and promoted the graphite mine. His second marriage in 1753 to Margaret Wynne was later to bring estates in North Wales to his grandson William. In 1762 he was appointed a Commissioner of Customs and in 1775 he employed the Customs Surveyor William Rice to build the offices in the laundry, later the kitchen, courtyard.

Henry Bankes the Younger (1757–1834), painted by Batoni in 1779 in Rome where he met his architect R. F. Brettingham, remodelled the house and married Frances Woodley in 1784. 'Mr Bankes of Corfe Castle' sat for Corfe from 1780 and then for Dorset from 1826 to 1831 as a stubborn independent Tory, the friend of William Pitt the Younger and the Duke of Wellington. 'Old Bankes' refused to stand again after losing his seat in 1831 for opposing reform. It is not clear how many pictures he added to the collection but he encouraged his son William whose acquisitions nearly all arrived during his lifetime. In 1815 he took his wife and younger daughter Maria on a 'trip to Paris before the Statues and Pictures are restored to their respective Countries'. He stocked his library with history and the classics and published in 1818 *A Civil and Constitutional History of Rome, from the Foundation to the Age of Augustus.* He died at Tregothnan, his son-in-law's seat in Cornwall, in December 1834. 'Mr Bankes was an accomplished scholar, intimately acquainted with ancient and modern literature, and of a refined and acknowledged taste in the arts, he was enabled to fulfill with peculiar grace his duties as one of the most active and zealous trustees of the British Museum, of which he was generally regarded as the organ and advocate in the House of Commons.'

William Bankes (1786–1855) was by far the most original of the Bankes family. 'My collegiate pastor, master and patron' who 'rules the Roast – or rather the Roasting – and was father of all mischiefs' wrote Byron of his Cambridge friend, whose rooms in Trinity are still decorated in the gothick taste with much Bankes heraldry. There he had an altar for burning incense where the choir boys chanted services, arousing suspicions of being a Catholic. After being MP for Truro from 1810–12, he won the Cambridge University seat in 1822 standing against Catholic Emancipation, when Macaulay called him 'our glorious, our Protestant Bankes'. From 1829–31 he sat for Marlborough and then for Dorset until 1835. But his heart was not in politics. After the blue-stocking heiress Annabella Milbanke rejected his proposal (she also turned down Byron at the time), he followed in the steps of Beckford and Byron to Portugal and Spain in 1812. He visited Wellington's headquarters after Salamanca but preferred the bohemian life in Granada where he was living 'in a beggarly eccentric fashion' in 1815.

He sent home his Spanish pictures and sailed for Egypt, making his first Nile journey lasting three months. He laid claim to the Philae obelisk and reached beyond Wadi Halfa. He engaged Giovanni Finati as guide and interpreter whose *Life and Adventures* he later translated and published in 1830. They joined Irby and Mangles in Jerusalem

Sir John Bankes, Lord Chief Justice,
by Gilbert Jackson

Sir Ralph Bankes, by Lely, the portrait at Yale

Henry Bankes the Younger by Batoni

William Bankes in 1836 by Hayter

and together with Thomas Legh of Lyme and Lord Belmore they explored east of the Dead Sea and made a daring expedition to Petra in Bedouin disguise. '. . . from his profound knowledge of ancient history as well as his skill in drawing, he was by far the best calculated to go on such an expedition', wrote his companions. Good at plans and architectural details, 'Bankes who leaves nothing unexplored' was a pioneer in Syria and also went to Palmyra and visited Lady Hester Stanhope on Mount Lebanon. His second, longer Nile journey lasted from October 1818 into the early summer of 1819, when he led Henry Salt's flotilla in his fourteen-oared boat. The British consul's party included Finati, Belzoni, and the artists Henry Beechey, Alessandro Ricci and the young Linant de Bellefonds, whose coloured drawings form the Bankes MSS at Kingston Lacy. They spent a month at Abu Simbel working half naked in very great heat by candlelight to copy the wall paintings inside the great temple of Rameses II. Charles Barry and his patron, Mr D. Ballie, met them on 13 January 1819 when 'I looked over Mr Bankes' drawings, which, on account of their great numbers, he kept in a basket'.

The following winter Bankes visited Byron in Venice, bought remarkable pictures in Bologna early in 1820 and 'buffooned together very merrily' with Byron for the last time in Ravenna before returning home in April after 'a narrow escape' crossing the Simplon. 'The Nubian explorer' was lionised by London society and even the normally hostile Samuel Rogers says 'witty as Sidney Smith was, I have seen him at

William Bankes in Oriental Dress attributed to Maxim Gauci, *c.*1820

Sir Charles Barry by John Hayter, 1838

my own house absolutely overpowered by the superior facetiousness of William Bankes'. He immediately set about rebuilding his Welsh house, Soughton, in Flintshire, where he was assisted by Barry but was largely 'his own architect' in the words of Barry's biographer, although the Islamic domed features on the forecourt wall are part of Barry's repertoire at Atree Villa, Brighton. This somewhat eccentric house was altered again in the 1860s after his death.

From 1835–41 he was engaged with Barry in rebuilding Kingston Hall. That year he was prosecuted for indulging in a homosexual act with a guardsman in a public place, jumped bail and fled to Italy. His affairs were administered by his brother George and Lord Falmouth but he retained his financial independence and continued to commission and send home works of art to furnish Kingston Lacy which remained his consuming passion up to the moment of his death.

George Bankes (1787–1856) restored an air of respectability to Kingston Lacy, which he looked after for fourteen years and then owned it only briefly. He married Georgina-Charlotte Nugent (whose real father, however, was the Duke of Cumberland, who became King of Hanover in 1837). They built a marine villa, the Manor House, at Studland. He was active in politics, especially during the controversy leading up to the Reform Bill, and was a Lord of the Treasury and the last Cursitor Baron of the Exchequer from 1824. 'George is but a poor judge in art, and has but an indifferent eye' William wrote in March 1855 to their sister Lady Falmouth who was living in

Ralph Bankes, donor of Kingston Lacy

Henrietta Jenny, Mrs W.R.Bankes

the house and on whom he relied for overseeing the decorations. George did, however, publish a book on the history of Corfe Castle, of which he was three times mayor when the Bankes' hereditary seat was abolished.

Of George Bankes' nine children, the third son won a posthumous v c at Lucknow, Edmund George the eldest outlived him by only four years, and *his* elder son died nine years after that aged nineteen. The estate then passed to Edmund George's other son, Walter Ralph Bankes (1853–1904), who inherited nearly thirty years before his marriage in 1897 to Henrietta Jenny Fraser. He was active on the estate, planting in the park and panelling the Dining Room after a fire, but the long Bankes tradition of parliamentary service had come to a close. His widow lived for another fifty years and recorded all her work on the estate and in the garden, building the Blandford and Wimborne lodges in 1912–13 and skilfully introducing bathrooms to the house in the 1920s. The house still reflects the style of 'Granny Bankes' today, especially in the Drawing Room. Her son, Ralph Bankes (1902–81), married Hilary Strickland-Constable in 1935 and bequeathed Corfe and Kingston Lacy to the nation.

Architectural History

The Restoration house was created for the gentry rather than the aristocracy, reflecting 'the politer way of living' noted by John Evelyn but domestic in character. It was mainly evolved by Roger Pratt (1620–84), the gentleman architect, and Hugh May, the friend of Lely, to house men of their own class in comfort, elegance and convenience and was based on the 'oblong square' house drawn by Inigo Jones and John Webb. Pratt returned from Italy in 1649 and was invited by his cousin to design his masterpiece, Coleshill, in the 1650s. In 1663 he designed Horseheath in Cambridgeshire, a larger and contemporary version of Kingston Lacy. More influential, because of its site in Piccadilly, was Lord Clarendon's town house of 1665 with its flanking wings. None of Pratt's houses have survived intact; his own home, Ryston Hall, Norfolk, of 1668–72 was, like Kingston Lacy, later transformed; Horseheath and Clarendon House were both short-lived and Coleshill was destroyed by fire in 1953.

Pratt's North Elevation of Kingston Hall

Plans of the Principal Floor of
Kingston Hall in the time of Roger
Pratt, 1663, and R.F.Brettingham, 1783.
Researched and drawn by Antony
Cleminson, Grad. Dipl. Cons. (AA)

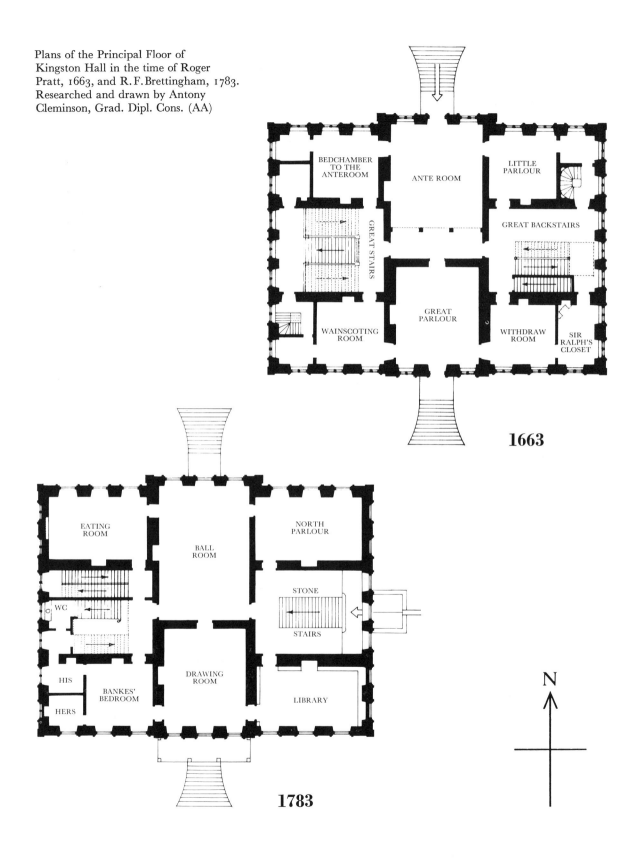

BEDCHAMBER
TO THE
ANTEROOM

ANTE ROOM

LITTLE
PARLOUR

GREAT STAIRS

GREAT BACKSTAIRS

WAINSCOTING
ROOM

GREAT
PARLOUR

WITHDRAW
ROOM

SIR
RALPH'S
CLOSET

1663

EATING
ROOM

BALL
ROOM

NORTH
PARLOUR

WC

STONE

STAIRS

HIS

HERS

BANKES'
BEDROOM

DRAWING
ROOM

LIBRARY

N

1783

The architect of Kingston Lacy, built from 1663 to 1665 or perhaps 1667, was forgotten until Pratt's notes, always very practical, were published in 1928. From these and from clues in the building itself, exposed in the recent restoration, the original plan is now clear. Only the smaller of Pratt's drawings for the north elevation now survives and shows the house as built, in red brick with stone quoins and mullion casement windows, a pediment with a marble coat of arms within a cartouche, and a hipped roof with dormer windows, crowned with a balustrade and a cupola. The house was entered directly on the principal floor or *piano nobile* up a flight of steps. The main rooms followed the old tradition of a double storey hall or anteroom with the great parlour beyond and the great chamber above it for dining with formality. On either side of the anteroom were the great stairs to the west and the great backstairs to the east. The former rose only to the bedchamber floor, but the latter led up to the great gallery running the length of the attic floor, another medieval survival, as at Thorpe Hall near Peterborough built in the 1650s. At the four corners of the house on two floors Pratt placed eight apartments, each consisting of a square room and one, or usually two, closets. (The closet partitions were self-supporting trusses on each floor and one can be seen exposed upstairs in the White Bedroom.) At bedchamber level the two ends of the house were connected by a wide balcony or '*pergolo*' running across the end of the anteroom and turning it into a cube, which probably also served to support the north side of the cupola. The profile of the '*pergolo*' was observed in its plaster shadow and two of the three characteristic Pratt sculpture niches survive bricked up over the blocked doorways.

John Bankes the Elder removed both cupola and '*pergolo*' in the early eighteenth century, when Pratt's great cornice was extended right round the anteroom. The listing of the rooms in the 1762 picture inventory shows that few other changes had taken place and when Hutchins published his *Dorset* in 1774 he showed the house without its cupola and balustrade.

It was always known that the house was almost rebuilt in the 1830s by Charles Barry (1795–1860) but only recent research and close observation have revealed the earlier transformation in the 1780s by Henry Bankes the Younger, who met his architect Robert Furze Brettingham in Rome. He also met Brettingham's companion, John Soane, who signed two drawings in 1779 for radical changes to the house which were not adopted. R. F. Brettingham probably wrote and asked his uncle, Matthew Brettingham the Younger, to provide the measurements of Kingston Hall for Soane and himself, because two of the three surviving floor plans are drawn on the back of ceiling proposals for Charlton Park near Malmesbury which Matthew Brettingham altered between 1772 and 1776. Soane came home in 1780 but R. F. Brettingham stayed in Rome until 1782 when Henry Bankes made a second visit.

The uncle's survey plans were altered to show the less sophisticated and less extensive changes carried out by the nephew. Italianate drawings in the archives also show proposals for altering the stairs and the rooms. In accordance with the current fashion,

Kingston Hall from the South by Neale, 1822

the kitchen went out of the house and the Dining Room came down to the principal floor. Placed in the north-west corner, this left Pratt's windswept entrance right next to the Dining Room door so a new main entrance was made at basement level in the stable yard, then still on the east side. Entering under a new Ionic porch, the visitor immediately climbed the new stone stairs to the centre of the house. Frances Bankes' report of her ball in 1791 confirms the plan of the principal floor, where Brettingham's Library and Saloon, with its coved ceiling painted by Cornelius Dixon and its Flaxman chimneypiece, survive. Mullioned windows were long out of date and sashes were introduced on all except the west elevation facing the kitchen yard. On the south front the sashes were even extended fashionably down to the floor level although the garden level was not raised, except that in front of the central Drawing Room a roofed arcaded pergola appeared, shown in Neale's engraving of 1822.

The new eating room (now the Spanish Room) was too small and no less than eight abortive proposals, notably by Thomas Cundy junior from 1819–24 and Jeffrey Wyatt in 1821, were considered for enlarging it (see page 31). Wyatt's scheme appears in an album of drawings for a somewhat clumsy transformation of the house, happily rejected. In October 1821 William Bankes wrote to his father of 'A young architect to whom I had been of what little use I could abroad, and to whom I had been lately able to do a pretty essential service in introducing and recommending him to Archdeacon Cambridge, who is one of the most active commissioners for the erection of new churches. . . . He is a very nice architectural draughtsman and therefore when I move into Dorsetshire I will have him down to Kingston Hall in order to have exact elevations and plans made of those alterations there which I have only roughly sketched upon paper, as well as to set him to contriving the distribution above stairs; that, whether executed or not, there may remain in evidence what were my notions upon the subject as confronted with those of Wyatt.'

Henry Bankes died in December 1834. From 1835 to William's flight abroad in 1841 Barry rebuilt the house for him and he was not an easy client, insisting on many ideas of his own which he followed through in the greatest detail. Kingston Hall, however, retained its original shape, although the entrance front, moved back to the north side at basement level, was given a vertical emphasis by lowering the ground by eight feet. By contrast the south side became more horizontal when the terrace was added. The house was encased in Chilmark stone, the attic storey was raised and a new balustrade and cupola provided, as well as tall corner chimneys as at Coleshill. Part of William's aim was to restore the house in the manner of Inigo Jones, whom

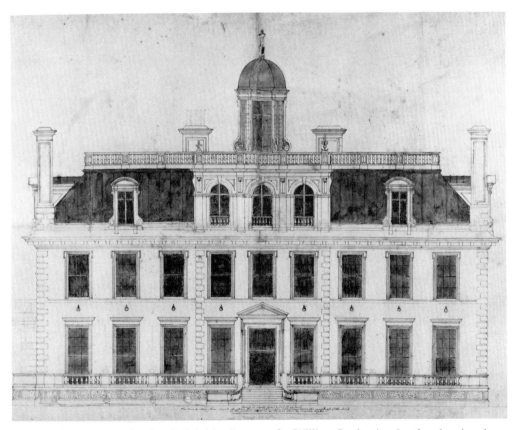

South Elevation 'drawn by Candlelight' by Seymour for William Bankes in 1849 for planning the Garden Ornaments

he supposed was Sir Ralph's architect, and internal features were borrowed from or inspired by Amesbury Abbey, Lees Court, the Queen's House at Greenwich and Coleshill, all visited either by him or Barry. Internally, the dining room problem was solved at some disturbance of the structure by throwing Brettingham's family stairs into the south-west apartment, and the ceilings here and in the Drawing Room were raised. The Marble Staircase on the east side is a *tour de force*, inspired by William. Among Barry's ideas are the eastern loggia and the internal Coffee Loggia. Over a hundred drawings from Barry's office are preserved in the house together with William's sketches and logbook of 1836–40 and detailed drawings and comments by Osborne his clerk of works and Seymour his mason.

Later he wrote an apologia for all this work, together with thirteen good reasons for remedying the defects and wants of the house. 'The house had continued to the third generation quite unaltered but the naturally timid disposition of my great uncle John Bankes induced him to remove the lantern altogether. . . . It came into my father's hands with no greater alterations than these and had it passed through his hands intact as it came into them I might have hesitated long about permitting myself to make any considerable change. It would have been interesting as a very complete and handsome specimen of the period and there were features in it that coupled with that impression that antiquity gives could not have failed to strike both as in themselves grand and as pictures of the life and manners of their days. The Great Hall especially with its Music Gallery and the broad staircase . . . would have been some palliative for present incommodiousness which I thought inadmissible in an altered house that was neither old nor modern in its character but a bad mixture of both.'

Anthony Mitchell 1987

Select Bibliography

The House

John Cornforth, in *Country Life*, 17, 24 April and 5, 12 June 1986.

Country Life, 21 April and 12 May 1900 and 16 April 1904.

Gardens Old and New, vol. I, *Country Life*.

R. T. Gunther, *The Architecture of Sir Roger Pratt*, 1928.

Oliver Hill and John Cornforth, *English Country Houses: Caroline*, 1966.

Rev. John Hutchins, *The History and Antiquities of the County of Dorset*, 1774.

The Ladies' Field, 2 June 1900.

Charles Lathom, *In English Homes*, vol. I, 3rd ed., 1909.

Arthur Oswald, *Country Houses of Dorset*, 1935.

Royal Commission on Historical Monuments, *County of Dorset*, vol. V, *East Dorset*, 1975.

Family History

ed. Francis Bamford and the Duke of Wellington, *The Journal of Mrs Arbuthnot*, 1950.

George Bankes, *The Story of Corfe Castle*, 1853 and *Brave Dame Mary*, 1873 and 1924.

Viola Bankes, *A Dorset Heritage: The Story of Kingston Lacy*, 1953 and 1986.

Viola Bankes, *A Kingston Lacy Childhood*, 1986.

A. L. Rowse, 'Byron's Friend Bankes: a Portrait', in *Encounter*, March 1975, and in *Homosexuals in History*, 1977.

Egypt

ed. W. J. Bankes, *Narrative of the Life and Adventures of Giovanni Finati*, 1830.

Jaroslav Černý, *Egyptian Stelae in the Bankes Collection*, 1958.

Peter A. Clayton, *The Rediscovery of Ancient Egypt*, 1982.

Nina M. Davies, *Egyptian Tomb Paintings*, 1958.

Warren R. Dawson and Eric P. Uphill, *Who was who in Egyptology*, 1972.

Eric Iversen, *Obelisks in Exile*, vol. II, 1972.

Kathleen MacLarnon, 'W. J. Bankes in Egypt', in *Apollo*, August 1986.

Pictures

R. B. Beckett, *Lely*, 1951.

Allan Braham, 'El Greco to Goya', introduction to exhibition catalogue, The National Gallery, 1981.

Enriqueta Harris, *Velasquez*, 1982, and in *The Burlington Magazine*, 1958 and July 1983.

Michael Hirst, *Sebastiano del Piombo*, 1981.

ed. Gervase Jackson-Stops, *The Treasure Houses of Britain*, exhibition catalogue, National Gallery of Art, Washington, 1985 (for Rubens, Titian and Velasquez).

The National Trust

for places of historic interest or natural beauty

This booklet describes one of over a thousand properties preserved for you by the National Trust.

Founded in 1895 the National Trust is today the greatest conservation society in Britain and the country's largest private landowner. It is not a government department: the Trust is a charity with membership open to everyone. It relies on the voluntary support of the public and the subscriptions, gifts and legacies of its members to maintain beautiful and unspoiled country and buildings of architectural or historic importance for your enjoyment and that of future generations.

The National Trust

Owns more than 200 houses of outstanding interest, many with fine collections of paintings, sculpture, furniture and porcelain; many gardens and some of the most beautiful examples of English landscape design; woods, moorland, hills and lakes, and nearly 500 miles of outstanding unspoilt coastline; some 1,100 farms; nature reserves including islands and fens; lengths of canal, wind- and water-mills, bridges and other industrial monuments; prehistoric and Roman antiquities; even whole villages;

Preserves them for your permanent enjoyment. In 1907 Parliament conferred upon the Trust the unique power to declare its land and buildings inalienable; and subsequent legislation gave it the right to appeal to Parliament against a compulsory purchase order on its inalienable land. Nearly all its properties are inalienable and this also means that they cannot be sold or mortgaged. If the Trust so wishes, and with approval of the Charity Commission, inalienable land can be leased;

Encourages free public access to all its country and coastline (subject to the interests of farming, forestry, wildlife and amenity) and opens more than 230 properties at a charge which helps the Trust to maintain them in a fitting manner. Entry is free to National Trust members;

Depends on the generosity of its friends and benefactors. The cost of maintaining, managing and opening a property to the public has risen sharply in recent years. Unless income can be steadily increased, there is bound to be a reduction in what the Trust can achieve. Please consider how you can help the Trust.

Membership

You can play a part in this great work of conservation by becoming a member of the National Trust. For details please ask at your nearest Trust property for our recruitment leaflet or write to the National Trust, Membership Department, P.O. Box 39, Bromley, Kent, BRI INH.

Gifts

The Trust welcomes donations to help finance its work. All gifts to the Trust are exempt from Inheritance Tax and Capital Gains Tax and as a charity we are able to recover income tax on covenanted gifts. For more information, write to: Appeals Manager, The National Trust, 36 Queen Anne's Gate, London, SWIH 9AS.

Legacies

Please consider leaving the Trust a legacy in your will and remember that in times of rising values and prices a bequest of the residue or a fraction of the residue of your estate would be a great help in enabling the Trust to keep pace with inflation.

The following are suitable forms of words to send to your solicitor with a request that they be included in your will. He will do the rest. You can tell him that as a charity all legacies to the Trust are exempt from tax.

'I bequeath the residue of my estate to the National Trust for Places of Historic Interest or Natural Beauty of 36 Queen Anne's Gate in the City of Westminster',

or 'I bequeath to the National Trust for Places of Historic Interest or Natural Beauty of 36 Queen Anne's Gate in the City of Westminster a share (state the fraction you choose) of the residue of my estate',

or 'I bequeath to the National Trust for Places of Historic Interest or Natural Beauty of 36 Queen Anne's Gate in the City of Westminster the sum of £ . . .'

The Solicitor to the National Trust at 36 Queen Anne's Gate, London, SWIH 9AS is always glad to advise prospective benefactors and their professional advisers on specific cases and will suggest suitable forms of words in any case not covered by the above, or will advise suitable wording for a codicil.